Introduction

By Fred Feldman

These writings and speeches by James P. Cannon express the revolutionary perspective that has motivated the American Trotskyist movement from its beginnings in 1928. The restatement and codification of these principles in the "Theses on the American Revolution," adopted at the Twelfth National Convention of the Socialist Workers party (SWP) in 1946, were spurred by the political situation that developed as a result of World War II.

The United States emerged from the war as the world's supreme capitalist power, with vast economic resources and sole possession of the atomic bomb. Publicists for the ruling class announced the coming of the "American Century" in which U.S. imperialism would hold sway over the globe.

Coinciding with the first signs of an economic boom in the United States, and with setbacks to the European revolution caused by Stalinism, this propaganda sparked a new crop of theories of "American exceptionalism." "American exceptionalism" is the concept that special characteristics of American capitalism, together with the organic backwardness of the American workers, render U.S. capitalism immune to the revolutionary crises that plague capitalism in the rest of the world. These views found an echo in the SWP, in a small faction headed by Albert Goldman and Felix Morrow.

At the same time, the American workers succeeded, by a massive strike wave, in beating back an assault by the employers and the Truman administration on the unions. This upsurge in militancy resulted in hundreds of workers joining the SWP. The Theses sought to provide these new members with a concise cummary of the basic revolutionary perspective and role of the party.

The "American Theses" predicted flatly that the "American Century" was doomed to failure. The deep roots that American imperialism had set down in world economy made it highly vulnerable at home to all the political and economic crises of a decaying world capitalist system. In building up its economic power, American capitalism had created its potential gravediggers in a huge, concentrated, and powerful working class. The high standard of living of these workers, relative to workers in other countries, need not be a reactionary force. The "American Theses" predicted that the desire to preserve this living standard would spur workers to militant struggle in the face of economic and social pressures. In a crisis, the American workers could assimilate the class struggle experience of workers all over the world and move rapidly onto the revolutionary stage.

The "American Theses" rejected schema about how the American workers would come to political class consciousness and revolutionary action. While continuing to advocate formation of a labor party based on the powerful union movement, the SWP did not regard it as inevitable that the American workers would go through a "stage" of reformism under the aegis of a labor party dominated by a Stalinist or Social Democratic leadership. More explosive variants could be envisaged, including the possiblity of rapid movement of the workers toward the revolutionary party itself.

The "American Theses" recognized that the American revolution will be the decisive battle of the world revolution. Victory can be assured only through the building of a mass revolutionary working class party. The indispensable nucleus of that party already exists in the Socialist Workers party, its program and its cadres.

This stance is a necessity for those who would build a revolutionary party. Although a party with a few hundred cadres, like the SWP in 1946, will necessarily carry out primarily propaganda tasks, its words and deeds must make it unmistakably clear that it seriously intends to become a mass workers party. A revolutionary nucleus which does not view its role in this way will never succeed in creating a mass revolutionary party.

Because of the international role of American imperialism, such a party can only be created as a component part of and in the closest political collaboration with the world revolutionary movement, the Fourth International.

The "American Theses" was not a conjunctural document. Its validity did not depend on the momentary ups and downs of the class struggle, but on the validity of a class-struggle perspective for the United States.

Other resolutions adopted at the 1946 SWP convention predicted that the workers upsurge in the U.S. would soon evolve into a revolutionary situation. This failed to materialize for three reasons: (1) the postwar revolutionary upsurge in Europe was aborted by the class-collaborationist policies of the Stalinists and Social Democrats; (2) on the basis of this betrayal, a new capitalist boom began in the advanced capitalist countries; and (3) the postwar anticommunist witch-hunt, culminating in McCarthyism, had a deeply conservatizing effect on political life in the United States.

The heavy blows dealt the revolutionary movement in this period affected the outlook of a section of the SWP membership. Under the leadership of Bert Cochran, George Clarke, and Mike Bartell, they challenged the basic programmatic perspectives contained in the "American Theses." They predicted that only the impact of a world war could shake the American workers out of their stupor. One wing of this faction held that the Reutherite wing of the union bureaucracy was more progressive than the American working class, while another rested its hopes on the Stalinists. It was in 1952, in the midst of this factional struggle, that Cannon wrote the letters on the "American Theses" that appear on pages 25-28 of this bulletin.

Since the Theses was adopted, the SWP has continued to evaluate new developments in the light of its basic perspective. The rise of student protests and of the women's liberation movement have been carefully studied. The most important addition to the SWP's strategy has been the recognition that the American revolution will have a combined character. The concentration, militancy, and proletarian composition of the Black population, and the social power and nationalist direction of its struggles have demonstrated that the coming revolution will be both an upheaval of the whole working class against capitalist exploitation and a struggle of the oppressed Black nationality for self-determination. A similar analysis has also been made with regard to the nationalist struggles of the Chicano nationality in the southwest United States. The combined character of the American revolution was codified in the political resolution passed by the 1969 SWP Convention, "The Course of U.S. Imperialism and the Revolutionary Struggle for a Socialist America," and in the political report by Jack Barnes to the February 1970 plenum of the SWP National Committee. These items are reprinted in *Towards an American Socialist Revolution* (New York: Pathfinder, 1971, $1.95).

The basic concepts of the "American Theses" were first put forward by Leon Trotsky in his writings on the American revolution. Selections from his writings appear as an appendix to this bulletin. As early as 1928, Trotsky wrote in his criticism of the draft program of the Comintern, "It is precisely the international strength of the United States and her irresistible expansion arising from it, that compels her to include the powder magazines of the whole world into the foundations of her structure, i.e., all the antagonisms between the East and the West, the class struggle in Old Europe, the uprisings of the colonial masses, and all wars and revolutions. On the one hand, this transforms North American capitalism into the basic counter-revolutionary force of the modern epoch, constantly more interested in the maintenance of 'order' in every corner of the terrestrial globe; and on the other hand, this prepares the ground for a gigantic revolutionary explosion in this already dominant and still expanding world imperialist power. The logic of world relations indicates that the time of this explosion cannot lag very far behind that of the proletarian revolution in Europe." (*The Third International After Lenin* [New York: Pathfinder, 1970, $3.45.])

Later, Trotsky was to state this position with even greater emphasis. In his first letter to the Communist League of America, published in the June 1, 1929, issue of the *Militant,* Trotsky wrote: "The work to be achieved by the American Opposition has international historic significance, for in the last historic analysis all the problems of our planet will be decided upon American soil. There is much in favor of the idea that from the standpoint of revolutionary order, Europe and the East stand ahead of the United States. But a course of events is possible in which this order might be broken in favor of the proletariat of the United States. Moreover, even if you assume that America which now shakes the whole world will be shaken last of all, the danger remains that a revolutionary situation in the United States may catch the vanguard of the American proletariat unprepared, as was the case in Germany in 1923, in England in 1926, and in China in 1925 to 1927. We must not for a minute lose sight of the fact that the might of American capitalism rests more and more upon a foundation of world economy with its contradictions and crises, military and revolutionary. This means that a social crisis in the United States may arrive a good deal sooner than many think, and have a feverish development from the beginning. Hence the conclusion: It is necessary to prepare."

1. Theses on the American Revolution

resolution adopted by the Twelfth National convention of the SWP, November 1946

I

The United States, the most powerful capitalist country in history, is a component part of the world capitalist system and is subject to the same general laws. It suffers from the same incurable diseases and is destined to share the same fate. The overwhelming preponderance of American imperialism does not exempt it from the decay of world capitalism, but on the contrary acts to involve it ever more deeply, inextricably, and hopelessly. U. S. capitalism can no more escape from the revolutionary consequences of world capitalist decay than the older European capitalist powers. The blind alley in which world capitalism has arrived, and the U. S. with it, excludes a new organic era of capitalist stabilization. The dominant world position of American imperialism now accentuates and aggravates the death agony of capitalism as a whole.

II

American imperialism emerged victorious from the Second World War, not merely over its German and Japanese rivals, but also over its "democratic" allies, especially Great Britain. Today Wall Street unquestionably is the dominant world imperialist center. Precisely because it has issued from the war vastly strengthened in relation to all its capitalist rivals, U. S. imperialism seems indomitable. So overpowering in all fields—diplomatic, military, commercial, financial, and industrial—is Wall Street's preponderance that consolidation of its world hegemony seems to be within easy reach. Wall Street hopes to inaugurate the so-called "American Century."

In reality, the American ruling class faces more insurmountable obstacles in "organizing the world" than confronted the German bourgeoisie in its repeated and abortive attempts to attain a much more modest goal, namely: "organizing Europe."

The meteoric rise of U. S. imperialism to world supremacy comes too late. Moreover, American imperialism rests increasingly on the foundations of world economy, in sharp contrast to the situation prevailing before the First World War, when it rested primarily on the internal market—the source of its previous successes and equilibrium. But the world foundation is today shot through with insoluble contradictions; it suffers from chronic dislocations and is mined with revolutionary powder kegs.

American capitalism, hitherto only partially involved in the death agony of capitalism as a world system, is henceforth subject to the full and direct impact of all the forces and contradictions that have debilitated the old capitalist countries of Europe.

The economic prerequisites for the socialist revolution are fully matured in the U. S. The political premises are likewise far more advanced than might appear on the surface.

III

The U. S. emerged from the Second World War, just as it did in 1918, as the strongest part of the capitalist world. But here ends the resemblance in the impact and consequences of the two wars upon the country's economic life. For in other major aspects the situation has in the meantime drastically altered.

In 1914-18 continental Europe was the main theater of war; the rest of the world, especially the colonial countries, was left virtually untouched by the hostilities. Thus, not only sections of continental Europe and England but the main framework of the world market itself remained intact. With all its European competitors embroiled in the war, the way was left clear for American capitalism to capture markets.

More than this, during the First World War capitalist Europe itself became a vast market for American industry and agriculture. The American bourgeoisie drained Europe of her accumulated wealth of centuries and supplanted their Old World rivals in the world market. This enabled the ruling class to convert the U. S. from a debtor into the world's banker and creditor, and simultaneously to expand both the heavy (capital goods) and the light (consumer goods) industries. Subsequently this wartime expansion permitted the fullest possible development of this country's domestic market. Finally, not merely did the American bourgeoisie make vast profits from the war but the country as a whole emerged much richer. The relatively cheap price of imperialist participation in World War I (only a few score billion dollars) was covered many times over by the accruing economic gains.

Profoundly different in its effects is the Second World War. This time only the Western Hemisphere has been left untouched militarily. The Far East, the main prize of the war, has been subjected to a devastation second only to that suffered by Germany and Eastern Europe. Continental Europe as well as England have been bankrupted by the war. The world market has been completely disrupted. Thus culminated the process of shrinking, splintering, and undermining that went on in the interval between the two wars (the withdrawal of one-sixth of the world — the USSR — from the capitalist orbit, the debasement of currency systems, the barter methods of Hitlerite Germany, Japan's inroads on Asiatic and Latin American markets, England's Empire Preference System, etc., etc.).

Europe, which defaulted on all its prior war and postwar debts to the U. S., this time served not as an inexhaustible and highly profitable market, but as a gigantic drain upon the wealth and resources of this country in the shape of lend-lease, overall conversion of American economy for wartime production, huge mobilization of manpower, large-scale casualties, and so on.

With regard to the internal market, the latter, instead of expanding organically as in 1914-18, experienced in the course of the Second World War only an artificial revival based on war expenditures.

While the bourgeoisie has been fabulously enriched, the country as a whole has become much poorer; the astronomic costs of the war will never be recouped.

In sum, the major factors that once served to foster and fortify American capitalism either no longer exist or are turning into their opposites.

IV

The prosperity that followed the First World War, which was hailed as a new capitalist era refuting all Marxist prognostications, ended in an economic catastrophe. But even this short-lived prosperity of the twenties was based on a combination of circumstances which cannot and will not recur again. In addition to the factors already listed, it is necessary to stress: (1) that American capitalism had a virgin continent to exploit; (2) that up to a point it had been able to maintain a certain balance between industry and agriculture; and (3) that the main base of capitalist expansion had been its internal market. So long as these three conditions existed — although they were already being undermined — it was possible for U. S. capitalism to maintain a relative stability.

The boom in the twenties nourished the myth of the permanent stability of American capitalism, giving rise to pompous and hollow theories of a "new capitalism," "American exceptionalism," the "American dream," and so forth and so on. The illusions about the possibilities and future of American capitalism were spread by the reformists and all other apologists for the ruling class not only at home but abroad. "Americanism" was the gospel of all the misleaders of the European and American working class.

What actually happened in the course of the fabulous prosperity of the twenties was that under these most favorable conditions, all the premises for an unparalleled economic catastrophe were prepared. Out of it came a chronic crisis of American agriculture. Out of it came a monstrous concentration of wealth in fewer and fewer hands. Correspondingly, the rest of the population became relatively poorer. Thus, while in the decade of 1920-30, industrial productivity increased by 50 percent, wages rose only 30 percent. The workers were able to buy — in prosperity — proportionately less than before.

The relative impoverishment of the American people is likewise mirrored in national wealth statistics. By 1928 the workers' share of the national wealth had dropped to 4.7 percent; while the farmers retained only 15.4 percent. At the same time, the bourgeoisie's share of the national wealth had risen to 79.9 percent, with most of it falling into the hands of the Sixty Families and their retainers.

The distribution of national income likewise expressed this monstrous disproportion. In 1929, at the peak of prosperity, *36,000 families had the same income as 11 million "lower-bracket" families.*

This concentration of wealth was a cardinal factor in limiting the absorbing capacity of the internal market. Compensating external outlets for agriculture and industry could not be found in a constricting world market.

Moreover, the need to export raw materials and agricultural products tended to further unbalance American foreign trade. This inescapably led to a further dislocation of the world market, whose participants were debtor countries, themselves in need of selling more than they bought in order to cover payments on their debts, largely owed to the U. S.

While appearing and functioning in the role of stabilizers of capitalism, the American imperialists were thus its greatest disrupters both at home and abroad. The U. S. turned out to be the main source of world instability, the prime aggravator of imperialist contradictions.

In the interim between the two wars this manifested itself most graphically in the fact that all economic convulsions began in the Republic of the Dollar, the home of "rugged individualism." This was the case with the first postwar crisis of 1920-21; this was repeated eight years later when the disproportion between agriculture and industry reached the breaking point and when the internal market had become saturated owing to the impoverishment of the people at one pole and the aggrandizement of the monopolists at the other. The Great American Boom exploded in a crisis which shattered the economic foundations of all capitalist countries.

V

The economic crisis of 1929 was not a cyclical crisis such as periodically accompanied organic capitalist development in the past, leading to new and higher productive levels. It was a major historical crisis of capitalism in decay, which could not be overcome through the "normal" channels; that is to say, through the blind interplay of the laws governing the market.

Production virtually came to a standstill. National income was cut into less than half, plummeting from $81 billion in 1929 to $40 billion in 1932. Industry and agriculture sagged. The army of unemployed swelled tenfold "normal," reaching the dizzy figure of 20 million. According to official estimates, based on 1929 averages, the losses in the years 1930-38 amounted to 43 million man years of labor, and $133 billion of national incomes.

By 1939 the national debt soared to $40 billion, or $14 billion more than the highest point at the end of the First World War. The number of unemployed kept hovering at 10 million. Industry and agriculture stagnated. The foreign trade of the U. S. in a reduced world market fell to less than half of its "normal" peacetime share.

What all these figures really express is the fearsome degradation of living standards of the workers and the middle class, and the outright pauperization of the "underprivileged one-third" of the population. The wafer-thin layer of monopolists, naturally, did not suffer at all, but on the contrary utilized the crisis in order to gobble up even a larger share of the country's wealth and resources.

The bourgeoisie saw no way out of the crisis. They had no way out. They and their regime remained the main obstacle in the way not only of domestic but of world recovery. In its downward plunge, the American bourgeoisie dragged the rest of the capitalist world with it, and kept it down.

Decisive is the fact that despite all the "pump-priming," "brain-trusting," and emergency "reforms," American capitalism was incapable of solving the crisis. The partial upswing of 1934-37 proved to be temporary and passing in character. The precipitous drop that occurred in 1937 revealed the abyss facing American capitalism. The threatening new downward plunge was cut off only by the huge expenditures made in preparation for the Second World War.

Only the war temporarily resolved the economic crisis which had lasted in both hemispheres for ten years. The grim reality, however, is that this "solution" has solved exactly nothing. Least of all did it remove or even mitigate a single one of the basic causes for the crisis of 1929.

VI

The basis of the current American postwar prosperity is the artificial expansion of industry and agriculture through unprecedented government spending which is swelling constantly the enormous national debt. In its fictitious character the war and postwar boom of the early forties far exceeds the orgy engaged in by European capitalism during 1914-18 and the immediate postwar years. The diversion of production into war industry on an unheard of scale resulted in temporary shortages of consumer goods. The home and foreign markets seemed to acquire a new absorbing capacity. Universal scarcities and war havoc are acting as temporary spurs to production, especially in the consumers' goods field.

Overall there is, however, the universal impoverishment, the disrupted economic, fiscal, and government systems — coupled with the chronic diseases and contradictions of capitalism, not softened but aggravated by the war.

If we multiply the condition in which European capitalism, with England at its head, emerged from the First World War by ten times and in some instances a hundred times — because of the vaster scale of the consequences of World War II — then we will arrive at an approximation of the actual state of American capitalism.

Every single factor underlying the current "peacetime" prosperity is ephemeral. This country has emerged not richer from the Second World War as was the case in the twenties, but poorer — in a far more impoverished world. The disproportion between agriculture and industry has likewise increased tremendously, despite the hothouse expansion of agriculture. The concentration of wealth and the polarization of the American population into rich and poor has continued at a forced pace.

The basic conditions that precipitated the 1929 crisis when American capitalism enjoyed its fullest health not only persist but have grown more malignant. Once the internal market is again saturated, no adequate outlet can be hoped for in the unbalanced world market. The enormously augmented productive capacity of the U. S. collides against the limits of the world market and its shrinking capacity. Ruined Europe herself needs to export. So does the ruined Orient, whose equilibrium has been ruptured by the shattering of Japan, its most advanced sector.

Europe is in dire need of billions in loans. In addition to lend-lease, Wall Street has already pumped almost $5 billion in loans into England; almost $2 billion into France; and smaller sums into the other satellite countries of Western Europe — without however achieving any semblance of stabilization there. Bankrupt capitalist Europe remains both a competitor on the world market and a bottomless drain. The Orient, too, needs loans, especially China, which, while in the throes of civil war, has already swallowed up as many American dollars as did Germany in the early twenties.

At home, the explosive materials are accumulating at a truly American tempo. Carrying charges on the huge national debt; the astronomic military "peacetime" budget ($18.5 billion for this year); the inflation, the "overhead expenditures" of Wall Street's program of world domination, etc., etc. — all this can come from one source and one only: national income. In plain words, from the purchasing power of the masses. Degradation of workers' living conditions and the pauperization of the farmers and the urban middle class — that is the meaning of Wall Street's program.

VII

The following conclusion flows from the objective situation: U. S. imperialism which proved incapable of recovering from its crisis and stabilizing itself in the ten-year period preceding the outbreak of the Second World War is heading for an even more catastrophic explosion in the current postwar era. The cardinal factor which will light the fuse is this: The home market, after an initial and artificial revival, must contract. It cannot expand as it did in the twenties. What is really in store is not unbounded prosperity but a short-lived boom. In the wake of the boom must come another crisis and depression which will make the 1929-32 conditions look prosperous by comparison.

VIII

The impending economic paroxyms must, under the existing conditions, pass inexorably into the social and political crisis of American capitalism, posing in its course pointblank the question of who shall be the master in the land. In their mad drive to conquer and enslave the entire world, the American monopolists are today preparing war against the Soviet

Union. This war program, which may be brought to a head by a crisis or the fear of a crisis at home, will meet with incalculable obstacles and difficulties. A war will not solve the internal difficulties of American imperialism but will rather sharpen and complicate them. Such a war will meet with fierce resistance not only by the peoples of the USSR, but also by the European and colonial masses who do not want to be the slaves of Wall Street. At home the fiercest resistance will be generated. Wall Street's war drive, aggravating the social crisis, may under certain conditions actually precipitate it. In any case, another war will not cancel out the socialist alternative to capitalism but only pose it more sharply.

The workers' struggle for power in the U. S. is not a perspective of a distant and hazy future but the realistic program of our epoch.

IX

The revolutionary movement of the American workers is an organic part of the world revolutionary process. The revolutionary upheavals of the European proletariat which lie ahead will complement, reinforce, and accelerate the revolutionary developments in the U. S. The liberationist struggles of the colonial peoples against imperialism which are unfolding before our eyes will exert a similar influence. Conversely, each blow dealt by the American proletariat to the imperialists at home will stimulate, supplement, and intensify the revolutionary struggles in Europe and the colonies. Every reversal suffered by imperialism anywhere will in turn produce ever greater repercussions in this country, generating such speed and power as will tend to reduce all time intervals both at home and abroad.

X

The role of America in the world is decisive. Should the European and colonial revolutions, now on the order of the day, precede in point of time the culmination of the struggle in the U. S., they would immediately be confronted with the necessity of defending their conquests against the economic and military assaults of the American imperialist monster. The ability of the victorious insurgent peoples everywhere to maintain themselves would depend to a high degree on the strength and fighting capacity of the revolutionary labor movement in America. The American workers would then be obliged to come to their aid, just as the Western European working class came to the aid of the Russian Revolution and saved it by blocking full-scale imperialist military assaults upon the young workers' republic.

But even should the revolution in Europe and other parts of the world be once again retarded, it will by no means signify a prolonged stabilization of the world capitalist system. The issue of socialism or capitalism will not be finally decided until it is decided in the U. S. Another retardation of the proletarian revolution in one country or another, or even one continent or another, will not save American imperialism from its proletarian nemesis at home. The decisive battles for the communist future of mankind will be fought in the U. S.

The revolutionary victory of the workers in the U. S. will seal the doom of the senile bourgeois regimes in every part of our planet, and of the Stalinist bureaucracy, if it still exists at the time. The Russian Revolution raised the workers and colonial peoples to their feet. The American revolution with its hundredfold greater power will set in motion revolutionary forces that will change the face of our planet. The whole Western Hemisphere will quickly be consolidated into the Socialist United States of North, Central, and South America. This invincible power, merging with the revolutionary movements in all parts of the world, will put an end to the outlived capitalist system as a whole, and begin the grandiose task of world reconstruction under the banner of the Socialist United States of the World.

XI

Whereas the main problem of the workers in the Russian Revolution was to maintain their power once they had gained it, the problem in the United States is almost exclusively the problem of the conquest of power by the workers. The conquest of power in the United States will be more difficult than it was in backwards Russia, but precisely for that reason it will be much easier to consolidate and secure.

The dangers of internal counterrevolution, foreign intervention, imperialist blockade, and bureaucratic degeneration of a privileged labor caste—in Russia all of these dangers stemmed from the numerical weakness of the proletariat, the agelong poverty and backwardness inherited from czarism, and the isolation of the Russian Revolution. These dangers were in the final analysis unavoidable there.

These dangers scarcely exist in the U. S. Thanks to the overwhelming numerical superiority and social weight of the proletariat, its high cultural level and potential; thanks to the country's vast resources, its productive capacity and preponderant strength on the world arena, the victorious proletarian revolution in the U. S., once it has consolidated its power, will be almost automatically secured against capitalist restoration either by internal counterrevolution or by foreign intervention and imperialist blockade.

As for the danger of bureaucratic degeneration after the revolutionary victory—this can only arise from privileges which are in turn based on backwardness, poverty, and universal scarcities. Such a danger could have no material foundation within the U. S. Here the triumphant workers' and farmers' government would from the very beginning be able to organize socialist production on far higher levels than under capitalism, and virtually overnight assure such a high standard of living for the masses as would strip privileges in the material sense of any serious meaning whatever. Mawkish speculations concerning the danger of bureaucratic degeneration after the victorious revolution serve no purpose except to introduce skepticism and pessimism into the ranks of the workers' vanguard, and paralyze their will to struggle, while providing fainthearts and snivelers with a convenient pretext for running away from the struggle. The problem in the U. S. is almost exclusively the problem of the workers' conquest of political power.

XII

In the coming struggle for power the main advantages will be on the side of the workers; with adequate mobilization of their forces and proper direction, the workers will win. If one wishes to deal with stern realities and not with superficial appearances, that is the only way to pose the question. The American capitalist class is strong, but the American working class is stronger.

The numerical strength and social weight of the American working class, greatly increased by the war, is overwhelming in the country's life. Nothing can stand up against it. The productivity of American labor, likewise greatly increased in wartime, is the highest in the world. This means skill, and skill means power.

The American workers are accustomed to the highest living

and working standards. The widely held view that high wages are a conservatizing factor tending to make workers immune to revolutionary ideas and actions is one-sided and false. This holds true only under conditions of capitalist stability where the relatively high standard of living can be maintained and even improved. This is excluded for the future, as our whole analysis has shown. On the other hand, the workers react most sensitively and violently to any infringement upon their living standards. This has already been demonstrated by the strike waves in which great masses of "conservative" workers have resorted to the most militant and radical course of action. In the given situation, therefore, the relatively high living standard of the American workers is a revolutionary and not, as is commonly believed, a conservatizing factor.

The revolutionary potential of the class is further strengthened by their traditional militancy coupled with the ability to react almost spontaneously in defense of their vital interests, and their singular resourcefulness and ingenuity (the sitdown strikes!).

Another highly important factor in raising the revolutionary potential of the American working class is its greatly increased cohesiveness and homogeneity — a transformation accomplished in the last quarter of a century. Previously, large and decisive sections of the proletariat in the basic industries were recruited by immigration. These foreign-born workers were handicapped and divided by language barriers, treated as social pariahs, and deprived of citizenship and the most elementary civil rights. All these circumstances appeared to be insuperable barriers in the way of their organization and functioning as a united labor force. In the intervening years, however, these foreign-born workers have been assimilated and "Americanized." They and their sons today constitute a powerful, militant, and articulate detachment of the organized labor movement.

An equally significant and profound development is represented by the transformation that has taken place in the position occupied by the Negroes. Formerly barred and deprived of the rights and benefits of organization by the dominant reactionary craft unions and, on the other hand, regarded and sometimes utilized by the employers as a reserve for strike-breaking purposes, masses of Negroes have since the twenties penetrated into the basic industries and into the unions. Not less than two million Negroes are members of the CIO, AFL, and independent unions. They have demonstrated in the great strike struggles that they stand in the front lines of progressiveness and militancy.

The American workers have the advantage of being comparatively free, especially among the younger and most militant layers, from reformist prejudices. The class as a whole has not been infected with the debilitating poison of reformism, either of the classic "Socialist" variety or the latter-day Stalinist brand. As a consequence, once they proceed to action, they more readily accept the most radical solutions. No important section of the class, let alone the class as a whole, has been demoralized by defeats. Finally, this young and mighty power is being drawn into the decisive phases of the class struggle at a tempo that creates unparalleled premises for mass radicalization.

XIII

Much has been said about the "backwardness" of the American working class as a justification for a pessimistic outlook, the postponement of the socialist revolution to a remote future, and withdrawal from the struggle. This is a very superficial view of the American workers and their prospects.

It is true that this class, in many respects the most advanced and progressive in the world, has not yet taken the road of independent political action on a mass scale. But this weakness can be swiftly overcome. Under the compulsion of objective necessity not only backward peoples but backward classes in advanced countries find themselves driven to clear great distances in single leaps. As a matter of fact, the American working class has already made one such leap which has advanced it far ahead of its old positions.

The workers entered the 1929 crisis as an unorganized, atomized mass imbued with illusions concerning "rugged individualism," "private initiative," "free enterprise," "the American Way," etc., etc. Less than 10 percent of the class as a whole was organized on the trade union field (fewer than 3 million out of 33 million in 1929). Moreover, this thin layer embraced primarily the highly skilled and privileged workers, organized in antiquated craft unions. The main and most decisive section of the workers knew unionism only as "company unionism," remaining without the benefit, the experience, and even the understanding of the most elementary form of workers' organization — the trade union. They were regarded and treated as mere raw material for capitalist exploitation, without rights or protection or any security of employment.

As a consequence, the 1929 crisis found the working class helpless and impotent. For three years the masses remained stunned and disoriented by the disaster. Their resistance was extremely limited and sporadic. But their anger and resentment accumulated. The next five years (1933-37), coincident with a partial revival of industry, witnessed a series of gigantic clashes, street fights and sit-down strikes — an embryonic civil war — the end result of which was a leap, a giant leap, for millions of workers from nonexistence as an organized force to trade union consciousness and organization. Once fairly started, the movement for unionism snowballed, embracing today almost 15 million in all the basic industries.

In one leap — in a brief decade — the American workers attained trade union consciousness on a higher plane and with mightier organizations than in any other advanced country. In the study and analysis of this great transformation, rather than in vapid ruminations over the "backwardness" of the American workers, one can find the key to prospective future developments. Under the impact of great events and pressing necessities the American workers will advance beyond the limits of trade unionism and acquire political class consciousness and organization in a similar sweeping movement.

XIV

The decisive instrument of the proletarian revolution is the party of the class conscious vanguard. Failing the leadership of such a party, the most favorable revolutionary situations, which arise from the objective circumstances, cannot be carried through to the final victory of the proletariat and the beginnings of planned reorganization of society on socialist foundations. This was demonstrated most conclusively — and positively — in the 1917 Russian Revolution. This same principled lesson derives no less irrefutably — even though negatively — from the entire world experience of the epoch of wars, revolutions, and colonial uprisings that began with the outbreak of the First World War in 1914.

However, this basic conclusion from the vast and tragic experience of the last third of a century can be and has been given a reactionary interpretation by a school of neo-revisionism, represented by the ideologues, philosophers, and preachers of prostration, capitulation, and defeat. They say in effect: "Since the revolutionary party is small and weak it is idle to speak of revolutionary possibilities. The weakness of the party changes everything." The authors of this "theory" reject and repudiate Marxism, embracing in its place the subjective school of sociology. They isolate the factor of the revolutionary party's relative numerical weakness at a particular moment from the totality of objective economic and political developments which creates all the necessary and sufficient conditions for the swift growth of the revolutionary vanguard party.

Given an objectively revolutionary situation, a proletarian party — even a small one — equipped with a precisely worked out Marxist program and firm cadres can expand its forces and come to the head of the revolutionary mass movement in a comparatively brief span of time. This too was proved conclusively — and positively — by the experiences of the Russian Revolution in 1917. There the Bolshevik Party, headed by Lenin and Trotsky, bounded forward from a tiny minority, just emerging from underground and isolation in February to the conquest of power in October — a period of nine months.

Numerical weakness, to be sure, is not a virtue for a revolutionary party but a weakness to be overcome by persistent work and resolute struggle. In the U.S. all the conditions are in the process of unfolding for the rapid transformation of the organized vanguard from a propaganda group to a mass party strong enough to lead the revolutionary struggle for power.

XV

The hopeless contradictions of American capitalism, inextricably tied up with the death agony of world capitalism, are bound to lead to a social crisis of such catastrophic proportions as will place the proletarian revolution on the order of the day. In this crisis, it is realistic to expect that the American workers, who attained trade union consciousness and organization within a single decade, will pass through another great transformation in their mentality, attaining political consciousness and organization. If in the course of this dynamic development a mass labor party based on the trade unions is formed, it will not represent a detour into reformist stagnation and futility, as happened in England and elsewhere in the period of capitalist ascent. From all indications, it will rather represent a preliminary stage in the political radicalization of the American workers, preparing them for the direct leadership of the revolutionary party.

The revolutionary vanguard party, destined to lead this tumultuous revolutionary movement in the U.S., does not have to be created. It already exists, and its name is the SOCIALIST WORKERS PARTY. It is the sole legitimate heir and continuator of pioneer American Communism and the revolutionary movements of the American workers from which it sprang. Its nucleus has already taken shape in three decades of unremitting work and struggle against the stream. Its program has been hammered out in ideological battles and successfully defended against every kind of revisionist assault upon it. The fundamental core of a professional leadership has been assembled and trained in the irreconcilable spirit of the combat party of the revolution.

The task of the SOCIALIST WORKERS PARTY consists simply in this: to remain true to its program and banner; to render it more precise with each new development and apply it correctly in the class struggle; and to expand and grow with the growth of the revolutionary mass movement, always aspiring to lead it to victory in the struggle for political power.

2. Report to the SWP Political Committee on the "Theses," October 4, 1946

reprinted from the October 1974 issue of *International Socialist Review*

These theses are the result of thoughts and informal discussions which have been taking place for a long time in our ranks. What is new about the theses is that for the first time we are sort of summing up and generalizing the ideas and perspectives which have governed our work for a long time—from the beginning as a matter of fact. As far as I know, all of our people both in the center and throughout the country have expressed agreement with them, which shows that the ideas are not new amongst us. What is new, I repeat, is that for the first time in generalized form an attempt is made to grapple with the perspectives of the revolution in the United States in a concrete manner.

Why is it necessary at this moment to bring this perspective forward? Well, first of all there is nothing artificial about it. All of our thoughts have been flowing together this way. The very fact that the theses met with universal approval in the leadership is an illustration of that. But there is an additional reason why it is especially timely right now. The attempt to build a revolutionary party in the United States, and to draw into it a mass of workers outside that very thin stratum of politically educated communists and socialists, requires an affirmation of a perspective. The workers who are called to join the party have got to be told in rather precise terms what this party is expected to accomplish. Not what it is fighting for as an ultimate and remote goal, but what is in store for them, what they can expect to achieve by their struggle. I think this is the only way you can ever build a revolutionary party on a broad basis—if you have a very clear view of your perspective and frankly state it.

Without having the theses, we have spoken more or less along these lines, and I have noticed—and perhaps you have—that the new workers who have been recruited into the party in the last couple of years take the revolutionary perspective very seriously. They understand what they are joining—a party that is going to make a revolution. There is much more revolutionary optimism among the new workers than there is in a lot of people who imagine themselves to be super-theoreticians, who haven't got any real faith in revolutionary possibilities in the United States. It is necessary now for our movement to state this precisely, and I believe it is necessary also for the sections of the Fourth International throughout the world. I believe that nothing can do more to lift them up and inspire them with new hopes; nothing can do as much as a declaration from the American party of its confidence in revolutionary prospects in the United States.

The theses represent a new stage, in my opinion, in the development of the concept of internationalism in America. If you go back through the history of the American movement, you can see that this concept of internationalism has gone through a process of evolution. Prior to the First World War the concept was rather nebulous, as were nearly all of the socialist ideas. The concept of internationalism as international solidarity, etc., was pretty strongly developed. What it meant in terms of revolution, what it meant in terms of the order in which the revolution would develop on a world scale, was never approached precisely.

The beginning of the Russian Revolution brought a new stage. It seemed as though the victory of the Russian Revolution in 1917 and subsequent years came at a time of the greatest reaction and the strongest upsurge of conservatism and prosperity in the United States. It was a pretty hardy Bolshevik who was able to see the prospects of revolution in the United States in the early years of the Russian Revolution. Our internationalism in those days could be expressed primarily as solidarity with the Russian Revolution—to support the Russian Revolution, defend the Russian Revolution. For example, one of the three main agitational slogans of the Communist Party in the early twenties was *recognition* of the Soviet Union by the United States.

By way of digression—to give you an idea of how far we have developed since that time—the three agitational slogans of the Communist Party in the early twenties were: Recognition of the Soviet Union; Amalgamation of the Craft Unions (and Organize the Unorganized, which was connected with that); and the Building of a Labor Party. Very elementary and very primitive.

So reactionary and conservative was the trade-union movement in those days that we didn't dare to hope for the organization of the unorganized as a revolutionary breaking up of the monopoly of the craft unions, but saw it only as the process of amalgamating them.

In 1928, as you know, we split with the Stalinists fundamentally over the question of internationalism. But it is interesting to note that the issues of our fight were not American. They dealt with the policy in the Soviet Union, the Anglo-Russian Committee,[1] the problems of the Chinese revolution; later on, the question of fascism in Europe, etc. Again, our internationalism, insofar as it expressed itself in practice, was that of a group outside the actual developments, fighting over and clarifying issues and questions dealing with other parts of the world, primarily with Europe and Russia and the Orient. It was not until the economic crisis broke in full force in the United States that the concept of revolutionary possibilities in this country began to interest rather wide circles of people. This crisis, which was a conjuncture, changed almost overnight the attitude of thousands and tens of thousands

1. The Anglo-Russian Trade Union Unity Committee was formed by Soviet and British union representatives in 1925. The British union bureaucrats used the prestige of their alliance with the Soviet government to bolster their authority in breaking the near-revolutionary general strike of 1926. Trotsky called for a public break with the committee but Stalin maintained the bloc until the British members, no longer needing it, walked out in 1927.

of people—especially among the intellectuals who generally react quicker than the mass of workers—toward American capitalism, which up to then had appeared to be completely invincible, not only to us but also to the Europeans.

The theses mention that marvelous honeymoon of the twenties when both here and throughout Europe, with the exception of the Bolsheviks, everyone was of the opinion that the American capitalist genius had solved the problems posed by Marx. In the early days of the crisis in the thirties there was a tremendous influx of intellectuals towards Marxism, or what they thought was Marxism. When capitalism showed its weaknesses most glaringly, they began to lose faith in it. They swelled the ranks of the Stalinist party and quite a few of them came to us.

Sometimes we are apt to forget that we had for a time almost a mass movement of Trotskyism, or pseudo-Trotskyism, in the radical intellectual circles in New York, which was based primarily on their reaction to the conjuncture of the crisis and their opinion—which was largely self-delusion—that they had become revolutionists and even Trotskyists. Suffice to recall that we had in the early thirties a fraction of New York high school and college teachers of between twenty and thirty members. We had a periphery of a hundred or two hundred intellectuals whom we counted on as sympathizers of Trotskyism. As you know, we don't have them today. The beginning of the economic upturn, combined with the events in Russia, Spain, and Europe generally, brought about a mass desertion of these people.

But even in that period of deepest crisis in America when the terrible cracks in the economic and social system were revealing themselves, it is important for us to remember that the big disputes in our party, in our movement here in the United States, the ones with which the great majority preoccupied themselves, were disputes over Russia, Spain, Germany, etc. The incipient split between the proletarian and the petty-bourgeois tendencies[2] was indicated in those days not so much by a formal and affirmative posing of questions as by the orientation each side took. The very fact that the proletarian tendency oriented itself very deeply toward the American labor movement and the trade unions, while the petty-bourgeois intellectuals preoccupied themselves almost entirely with foreign affairs was, so to speak, an unformulated beginning of a fundamental difference of conception of the role of our party and its potentialities on the American scene. We were acting according to these theses before we really formulated them as concretely as we have done today.

I said these theses should have a profound effect on the thinking, and especially on the morale, of the sections of the Fourth International. The shadow of this terrible power of American imperialism is undoubtedly very heavy over every section everywhere. France, Italy, England, South America—wherever it may be—the revolutionary workers of the Fourth International cannot fail to feel that they have not only the problem of overthrowing their own bourgeoisies, which they may feel fully competent they can do; they must feel that "this alone will not guarantee us anything because we will have to fight this colossus in North America." And I don't think anything can do more to round out and clarify their thoughts and struggle and morale than a positive assertion by the American party that we see the prospects of revolution in the United States and that we are organizing for that. That we are not playing the role of mere commentators on affairs in Europe and we are not going to be a Red Cross society to collect funds for someone else to make a revolution somewhere else, but our main contribution to the European movement is the making of a revolution in the United States which aims at victory.

These theses in their theoretical part are strictly Trotskyist. There isn't any innovation there. And I say Trotskyist in the sense of expressing the real thought and conviction of the Old Man himself. That goes way back. In the recent period I have been studying his writings from this point of view and it is remarkable how far back Trotsky, above all, saw the Achilles heel of this apparently invincible monster in the United States. At the Third Congress of the Comintern in 1921, referring to the feverish development of the American economy during the war and afterward, he expressed the opinion that it was bound to lead to a convulsive crisis. And he used the expression, as I recall it, that the revolutionary development of the American workers can proceed at an American tempo equal to its feverish economic development during the war and postwar period.

In 1929, in the first letter he sent to the Communist League of America from Constantinople, he said there were many indications that America would not be the first country to follow the example of the Russian Revolution. In fact it was rather common in those days to say and to think that America would be the last—that following Russia there would come Germany; it would spread over Europe and from Europe to the Orient, interacting on each other, and that America would be the last capitalist country to succumb to revolution. The Lovestoneites[3] put a decoration on top of that with

2. In 1940 a faction of the Socialist Workers Party led by Max Shachtman, James Burnham, and Martin Abern succumbed to the pressures of the impending entry of the United States into World War II. After the Stalin-Hitler Pact they repudiated the Trotskyist position of defending the Soviet Union against imperialist attack despite its leadership. They split from the SWP, taking with them most of the party's intellectual and student members, to form the Workers Party, which survived until the mid-1950s when it was dissolved into the Socialist Party of Norman Thomas.

3. When Stalin imposed his regime over the American Communist Party in the late 1920s the party was divided into three factions: the followers of Cannon who declared for Trotsky in 1928 and were expelled; the backers of William Z. Foster, who acquiesced in the Stalinist bureaucratization; and the supporters of Jay Lovestone, who were allied with the conservative Bukharin tendency in the Russian party and the Communist International. Expelled from the CP in 1929, the Lovestoneites commanded a sizable organizational force on the American left throughout the 1930s. At the outbreak of World War II they veered sharply to the right, dissolved their organization, and sought posts in the union movement. Lovestone became George Meany's assistant for international affairs in the AFL-CIO hierarchy.

their theory of "American exceptionalism," which in essence amounted to the idea that America was outside of revolutionary developments for a whole epoch. But in that first letter Trotsky said that while there was much to indicate that America would not be the first, a course of development would be possible in which this order would be sharply reversed and America could take first line in the revolutionary process.

From that point of view, he said, it was necessary to prepare a party with that in mind. The Transitional Program of 1938[4] — it is very interesting now in retrospect to recall the origin of this document — was written in Mexico after consultation and to a certain extent collaboration with a delegation from the United States. And at that time, I venture to say, the Old Man's main preoccupation already was with America, and he intended the Transitional Program as applicable to America as well as to Europe. The Transitional Program does not have any meaning unless one has in mind a revolutionary perspective. The very fact that you go over from the concept of the maximum and the minimum program — that is, the minimum program of daily small change, the maximum program of ultimate goal that you talk about on Sunday — to a transitional program presupposes a development of a revolutionary nature, with the prospects of a showdown struggle in sight. And the Transitional Program applies to America. As a matter of fact, if you recall the conversations and articles of the Old Man, I think he wrote more about America in its relation to the Transitional Program than about any other country.

Again, in his introduction to *The Living Thoughts of Karl Marx*[5] he develops very categorically the theme that America is heading toward great revolutionary explosions and to a revolution. More than once, confronted with the sweep of fascist reaction in Europe — which all those people who thought of internationalism and revolution solely in European terms took to be a sort of death sentence on the European movement — Trotsky said, "If fascism conquers Europe, then that means only that the center of Marxism will be transferred to American soil, and that the revolution in the United States would establish a new balance."

So from the point of view of the teachings of Trotsky and of the ideas by which we have been operating without stating so in precise terms, there is nothing new in the theses except that it is all brought together and generalized. But I believe it will be something new in its effect on the work of the party, and should be. The theses should be the starting point of a complete reorientation of our agitational and propaganda work. The whole party and its periphery and all the new recruits should be saturated with the ideas outlined in this document.

Just as in the early days of our movement — at least in the first ten years — we rearmed the movement with education and discussion and agitation around the basic principles of the Russian Opposition, the Anglo-Russian Committee, the policy in the Soviet Union, problems of the Chinese revolution, later on the problems of fascism in Europe, so now I believe we should go through that same process again of organizing our educational work, our literary and propagandistic work, in terms of popularizing and expanding on each one of the basic ideas gathered together here in the theses, so the whole party becomes saturated with the concept of the theses and the whole outlook that flows from it — that we are actually building a party to make the revolution in the United States.

Not the least of the results of the adoption of this document and the reorientation that will follow from it — the clarification of everything hazy as to what we mean, what we are driving at, what we hope to accomplish — is that it will bring out more clearly and fundamentally than ever the irreconcilable difference between us and the Mensheviks of all shades, including the Shachtmanites and our minority.[6] During the summer, while we were discussing these ideas and formulating some of them out in California, Murry and Charlie Curtiss[7] and I took occasion to study very attentively the bulletins of the Shachtmanites to see to what extent they have occupied themselves with this question of the perspectives of the American revolution. And it is really astonishing to see that they haven't given it a thought. They are far more interested in Stalinism and the national question in Europe. In fact, they are almost exclusively interested in that. Their resolution on the American question does not go any farther than we went in the heights of capitalist prosperity in the twenties, before the crisis — that is, of speculating on the next turn in the conjuncture and drawing some small-change conclusions with regard to tactics.

Johnson,[8] who brought in a counter-document in which he, in his own way, tried to assert that the Transitional Program has application for America and that there are

---

4. The Transitional Program, the full title of which is *The Death Agony of Capitalism and the Tasks of the Fourth International*, was written by Trotsky in 1938 as the founding platform of the Fourth International. It is available in the book *The Transitional Program for Socialist Revolution* (New York: Pathfinder Press, 1974).

5. Philadelphia: David McKay, 1939. This book is now out of print, but Trotsky's essay is available in pamphlet form under the author's original title, *Marxism in Our Time* (New York: Pathfinder Press, 1970).

6. Cannon is referring here to a minority faction organized by Albert Goldman and Felix Morrow, two long-time leaders of the SWP who were both imprisoned in the Minneapolis case. Goldman had been the party's attorney in the Minneapolis trial; Morrow was a writer and had been editor of *The Militant* and of *Fourth International* magazine, the predecessor of the *International Socialist Review*. While in prison they became disillusioned with the prospects for socialism and left the party in 1946.

7. Murry Weiss and Charles Curtiss were leaders of the Los Angeles branch of the SWP.

8. J.R. Johnson was a political pseudonym for the well-known West Indian writer C.L.R. James. He was a member of the SWP in the 1930s. He developed the position that the Soviet Union was a form of "state capitalism" and left the party with the Shachtmanites in 1940. He rejoined the SWP for a brief period at the end of the 1940s.

revolutionary perspectives in the foreseeable future in America, was just laughed out of court by the Shachtmanites. They don't ever see it; they don't think about it. It is noteworthy that our own soul-sick Mensheviks have never given that a thought, and that is one reason why they are so pessimistic, why they are crawling under the bed. It has never entered their heads, evidently, that the American working class can compensate in one or two blows for any number of defeats in Europe. And it is interesting also that our conflict with them on secondary questions — I don't think this has been formulated before, we have only felt but haven't stated it — had at its root a difference of perspective and goals in the United States.

We have always believed in the American revolution, and it is from that concept — even though we did not generalize it — that we derived our conception of the party: for example, of a revolutionary combat party, of a professional leadership, of an optimistic morale, of harsh demands upon the membership. Goldman, and later Morrow, and others attack us on these derivative conceptions. They are against the homogeneous party. They are against this combat nonsense. They are against discipline. Morrow, at the last plenum, called our revolutionary exhortations "dope." We dope up the party with fantasies, etc. Now, if you stop to think about it, this debate about the conception of the party is a rather sterile debate if you isolate it from your milieu and your perspective. If socialism is only a remote aspiration, a moral ideal, or an ultimate goal that you hope for as men of good will hope for the moral regeneration of the world, what in the hell do you want a tightly disciplined combat party with a professional leadership for? It becomes a caricature.

As a matter of fact, you couldn't have organized such a party as this in America before the First World War. The prospect of the final struggle for the dictatorship of the proletariat was so far off that it seemed like playing soldiers to have that kind of a party. On the other hand, if you foresee a development of the class struggle that is leading to revolutionary collisions and a fight for power, then our conception of the party flows very logically and necessarily from that. It is not accidental that the one place where a Leninist type of party was organized before the First World War was in Russia, because the Russians, especially the Bolsheviks, expected a revolution, and Lenin was preparing a party to lead a revolution. The Social Democrats in Europe, who had a perspective of long, drawn-out evolutionary development, saw no need of such a party.

Trotsky remarked in his autobiography that the difference between the Bolsheviks (which included Trotsky in this respect) and many others stemmed from the fact that there developed in the socialist movement, after one generation had succeeded another, a tendency toward conservatism of outlook as to prospects. People who recognized socialism as a desirable and eventually inevitable outcome postponed it to future generations, and that affected the whole life and concept of the party, its daily work, etc. The thing that characterized the Bolsheviks is that they were deliberately preparing for a revolution, and from that, as a derivative, flowed their type of party, their morale, etc.

You may say that, for all these years that we have been fighting both openly and in a muffled form with the petty-bourgeois tendency in our movement, we have been fighting over derivatives of a fundamentally different view of prospects in the United States, and all we are doing now is turning things upside down, or rather, right side up, and developing our revolutionary perspective from which we derive our conception of professional leadership, the heavy demands we make upon ourselves and others, etc.

I had a discussion with Comrade Dobbs just before the meeting about section XI [of the theses], which deals with the question of what the real problem in the United States is — whether it is a question of the struggle for power or the danger of bureaucratic degeneration afterwards. I believe that has to go in there because the common argument of all varieties of Menshevism is the danger and the possibility — or, as they think, the certainty — that the revolution, once achieved by our program, will go the way of the Russian Revolution. Munis[9] even wrote, incredible as it may seem, in an article, purportedly dealing with the most fundamental questions of the revolution, which was reprinted by Shachtman, that the fundamental problem is the prevention of Thermidorian reaction after the revolution. That is the theme upon which all our opponents harp — that the program of communism leads to totalitarian tyranny as in Russia. I think it is necessary to state in our theses, with the object of arming our comrades and new recruits in advance with the conception, that the problem in the United States is the problem of the conquest of power; that the danger confronting the American workers is that they won't take the power when the time comes, not that the power will degenerate, as in Russia, afterwards.

There is a section in thesis XV about the labor party which Comrade Dobbs also raised, in which he expressed the opinion that we state perhaps too categorically that a mass labor party based on the unions would arise. I would agree to make that a bit more qualified, to say that if in the course of this development there will be a mass labor party, etc., without giving the impression that we consider this a necessary and inevitable phase of development. I personally do not consider this inevitable at all. Another course of action is possible. If the growth of a labor party is delayed too long and the SWP continues to grow and expand, another development is possible. It is only the most probably indicated one at the present time.

There is the question also of the necessity of a program or thesis on the tremendous anti-red campaign that is developing. It might be argued against the theses that a new wave of repressions is being prepared: J. Edgar Hoover's speech at the American Legion convention; Attorney General Clark's speech before some lawyer's organization in Chicago in which he called for a tough attitude against red lawyers, which might indicate that they're all prepared for a new series of prosecutions; and the press campaign which encompasses practically the whole press and at least the AFL bureaucracy. It might be argued that a big wave of persecution would alter

9. Grandizo Munis was a Spanish Trotskyist. He participated in the civil war against Franco and in 1939 went into exile in Mexico. He later developed ultraleft and sectarian positions and left the Fourth International.

this perspective. We have to have a section in the document, if only a small one, asserting that our perspective is not based on the contemporary policy of the ruling class but upon more fundamental considerations of the weakness of the system economically and that it cannot be changed by persecutions — as a matter of fact, might be even accelerated by them. We must not concede at any place or any point to that school of thought now very popular among our neo-revisionists that revolutionary possibilities are decided by subjective factors — the existence or nonexistence, the strength or weakness of the party, or the reactionary or liberal policies of the ruling class at a given moment, etc. The revolutionary perspective of the Russian Revolution was not based upon a liberal regime and was not arrested by the most reactionary tsarist regime; and I believe it is necessary to have perhaps a small section stating that; that even if we encounter really ferocious persecution — and that seems more likely than not — that will not halt revolutionary developments or succeed in breaking up the party.

The point about the assertion of the role of the SWP, I think, follows from everything written in the document before. I think nothing condemns a party more than a lack of faith in its own future. I don't believe it is possible for any party to lead a revolution if it doesn't even have the ambition to do so. That is the case with the Shachtmanites and the case with Goldman and Morrow. The Shachtmanites assert that neither their party nor ours is the party of the future revolution. Somewhere, somehow, out of something or other, it will arise, they hope.

We must assert as a matter of course that our party is going to lead the revolution.

3. The Coming American Revolution

reprinted from *Speeches for Socialism* (New York: Pathfinder, 1971)

report to the November 1946 SWP convention on the "Theses"

We have undertaken as our central task at this twelfth convention of the Socialist Workers Party to analyze the present stage in the development of United States imperialism as it emerged from the Second World War — and its further perspectives — and to draw the necessary conclusions from this analysis.

In our main thesis we deal exclusively with the perspectives of the American revolution. Secondary questions of tactics, and even of strategy, are left for consideration under another point on the agenda after we have discussed and decided the main question of perspective.

The question might be asked: Why are the theses on perspectives needed now? In order for the party to see clearly on the road ahead it is necessary to have a main orientation and a long-range view of future developments. The theses we have presented are needed at the present moment for a number of reasons.

First, the whole Trotskyist concept of our epoch as the epoch of revolutions, has been challenged by a new school of revisionists of Marxism. What answer do we give to this challenge, with specific reference to the United States of America?

What conclusions do we draw from the war and its consequences; from the new power of American imperialism; from the postwar prosperity; and from the retardation of the European revolution? What conclusions do we draw from these great events for the conduct of our own work and for our own future outlook in the United States?

Secondly, what shall we say to our cothinkers in other lands about revolutionary prospects in the United States? They are surely waiting to hear from our convention on this question, for it is of the most vital and decisive importance for them. This applies to the workers of Europe, but not only to them. It applies to the workers of Russia, of South and Central America, of China, Japan, Asia as a whole, India — in fact, to the workers of the whole world which lies today under the shadow of American imperialism.

And finally, what shall the party teach the new members who today are streaming into our ranks by hundreds and who will come to us tomorrow in thousands? What shall we tell them concretely about the prospects of the revolution in the United States? That is what they want to know above everything else.

Our document undertakes to give straight answers to all these questions.

Another question may well be asked: What is new in the "Theses on the American Revolution" presented by the National Committee?

In one sense it can be said that nothing is new; for all our work has been inspired by, and all our struggles with opportunist tendencies have been derived from, a firm confidence on our part in the coming victory of the American workers.

In another sense it can be said that everything is new; for in the theses of the National Committee on the American revolution we are now stating, explicitly and concretely, what has always been implied in our fights with opportunist organizations, groups and tendencies over the questions which were derivative from this main outlook of ours.

That has been the underlying significance of our long struggle to build a homogeneous combat party. That has been the meaning of our stubborn and irreconcilable fight for a single program uniting the party as a whole; for a democratic and centralized and disciplined party with a professional leadership; for principled politics; for the proletarianization of the party composition; for the concentration of the party on trade-union work ("trade unionization of the party"); and, if I may say so without being misunderstood, for its "Americanization." All of this derived from our concept of the realism of revolutionary prospects in America, and of the necessity to create a party with that perspective in mind.

In short, we have worked and struggled to build a party fit to lead a revolution in the United States. At the bottom of all our conceptions was the basic idea that the proletarian revolution is a realistic proposition in this country, and not merely a far-off "ultimate goal," to be referred to on ceremonial occasions.

I say that is not new. In fact, it has often been expressed by many of us, including Trotsky, in personal articles and speeches. But only now, for the first time, has it been incorporated in a programmatic document of the party. That's what is new in our "Theses on the American Revolution." We are now stating explicitly what before was implied.

For the first time, the party as a party is posing concretely the fundamental question of the perspectives of the American revolution.

You will note in your reading of the theses that secondary questions of tactics and even of strategy, with all their importance, are left out. And this is not by accident or negligence, but by design. The theses deal only with analysis and perspectives — and these only in the broadest sense — *because that is the fundamental basis from which we proceed.*

Tactical questions and even questions of great strategical importance — such as the alliance of the labor movement and the Negro people, the role of the returned war veterans, the relations between the workers and the poor farmers and the urban petty bourgeoisie, the questions of fascism and of the labor party — these questions with all their great subordinate importance are left out of the main theses for separate consideration in other documents. They will be considered at another time in the convention, because the correct answer to all of them depends in reality on a correct answer to the main question of general perspective posed in the theses of the National Committee.

Of course, a general line, a general perspective, does not guarantee that one will always find the right answer to the derivative questions, the secondary issues. But without such a general orientation, without this broad overall ruling conception, it is quite hopeless to expect to find one's way in tactical and strategical questions.

The theses have been criticized already by people who deal exclusively in "the small coin of concrete events." We have been criticized because we "do not mention concrete tasks" and "pose no concrete problems."

That is true. But what is wrong with that procedure? We are Marxists; and therefore we do not begin with the small questions, with the tactics, or even with the strategy. We first lay down the governing line from which the answers to the secondary questions derive.

Those who preoccupy themselves primarily with tactics reproach us for our procedure, and allege that it reveals the difference between their political *method* and ours. That is quite correct. We proceed from the fundamental to the secondary; they proceed by nibbling at the secondary questions in order to undermine the fundamental concepts. There is indeed a difference in method.

Our theses specifically outline the revolutionary perspectives in America and require the party to conduct and regulate all its daily activity in light of these perspectives.

Our preoccupation at this convention with American affairs and American perspectives does not signify a departure on our part from the time-honored internationalism that has always distinguished our tendency. Rather, we are taking a step forward in the application of our internationalist concepts to American affairs. That means to bring them down from the realm of abstraction and give them flesh and blood.

We began in 1928 with a struggle for internationalism against the dogma of "socialism in one country" which had been imposed on the Comintern and all its sections by the Stalinist revisionists. That was the most fundamental of all the principled questions which have shaped and guided the development of our movement in America for the past eighteen years.

We said then, and we still believe, that the modern world is an economic unit; and that not a single important social problem — and certainly not the most important problem, the socialist reorganization of society — can be definitively solved on national grounds.

With the presentation of the theses of the National Committee on the perspectives of the American revolution, we are adding a correlative idea to the following effect: it is no longer possible to speak seriously about the world socialist revolution without specifically including America in the program. Today that would be almost as utopian as was the theory of "socialism in one country" when it was first promulgated by Stalin for Russia in 1924.

This was always true, but it is truer now than ever in the light of the Second World War and its outcome. The United States has emerged from the war as the strongest power in the world, both economically and militarily. Our theses assert that the role of the United States in further world developments will be decisive in all respects.

If the workers in another country, or even in a series of other countries, take power before the revolutionary victory in the United States, they will have to defend themselves against the American colossus, armed to the teeth and counterrevolutionary to the core.

On the other hand, a revolutionary victory in the United States, signalizing the downfall of the strongest bastion of capitalism, would seal its doom on an international scale.

Or, in a third variant, if the socialist revolution should be defeated in other countries or even on other continents, and pushed back and retarded, we can still fight and win in the United States. And that would again revive the revolution everywhere else in the world.

The world situation makes it quite clear that platonic internationalism is decidedly out of date in this country. Internationalism, as the Trotskyists have conceived it, means first of all, international collaboration. But in our view this international collaboration must signify not only the discussion of the problems and tasks of cothinkers in other countries — this is where platonic internationalism begins and ends — but also the solution of these problems, above all our own specific problems, *in action.* That is our conception of internationalism as we mean to apply it and as we have expressed it in the theses.

One-sided internationalism — preoccupation with far-off questions to the exclusion and neglect of the burning problems on one's own doorstep — is a form of escapism from the realities at home, a caricature of internationalism. This simple truth has not always been understood, and there are some people who do not understand it yet. But our party can justify its existence only if, beginning with an international program, it succeeds in applying this program to the conditions of American life and confirming it in action.

This presupposes first of all an attentive study of America and a firm confidence in its revolutionary perspectives. Those who are content with the role of commentators on foreign affairs — and it is surprising how many there are — or that of a Red Cross society to aid other revolutions in other countries, will never lead a revolution in their own country; and in the long run they will not be of much help to other countries either. What the other countries need from us, above everything else, is one small but good revolution in the United States.

Trotskyism — which is only another name for Bolshevism — is a world doctrine and concerns itself with all questions of world import. But let us not forget — or rather, let some of us begin to recognize for the first time — that America, the United States, is part of the world; in fact, its strongest and most decisive part, whose further development will be most fateful for the whole.

It is from this point of view that we deem it necessary now to outline more concretely and more precisely than before our estimation of American perspectives, and to concentrate on the preparation for them. When we speak of the "Americanization" of the party in this sense we are not speaking as vulgar nationalists — far from it — but as genuine internationalists of the deed as well as of the word.

Our theses on the perspectives of the American revolution proceed in accord with the Marxist method and the Marxist tradition by analyzing and emphasizing first of all the objective factors that are making for the revolution. *These are primary. These are fundamental.* Any other approach than that which begins with the objective factors is unrealistic, mere wishful-thinking utopianism, no matter how revolutionary-minded its proponents may be.

This characterization of unrealism applies also to the new revelation of those who have exalted the subjective factor — meaning thereby the party and its strength or weakness at the given moment — to first place.

It would be incorrect, however, to add the supplementary qualification that these latter-day experts of the subjective factor, these latter-day revisionists, are "revolutionary-minded." They are unrealistic, but not revolutionary-minded, for they employ their new "theory" exclusively for the explanation of past defeats and anticipation and prediction of new ones. I don't see anything revolutionary about that.

Our theses pay due acknowledgment to the great strength of United States imperialism. Let no one accuse us of failing to give the American imperialist power its due. We paid due acknowledgment to it. This is correct and proper in a document which aims at scientific objectivity; for the might and resources of the Yankee colossus are so imposing in relation to all other countries, and in relation to anything that has ever been seen in the world before in the realm of material power — and have been so well advertised in the bargain — that no one could possibly overlook them.

But our theses — and here we demarcate ourselves from all those who are hypnotized by the superficial appearance of things — point out not only the strength of American imperialism but also its inherent weaknesses; the contradictions from which it cannot escape; and the new, even greater, power which it has created and which is destined to be its gravedigger — the American working class. That is also part of the American picture which has to be observed and noted if one wants to have a completely true and objectively formulated document.

A one-sided view of the American capitalist system — overestimation of its power and awestruck prostration before it — is the source of many illusions. And these illusions, in turn, are the chief source of American labor opportunism in general; of the capitulation and treachery of the radical intellectuals en masse; of Stalinism; and of all varieties of reformism and Menshevism.

In considering the perspectives of the American capitalist system in general and of the present postwar prosperity in particular, we observe a peculiar and rather interesting anomaly. The capitalist masters of society, and their ideologues and economic experts, enter the new period with doubts and fears which they do not conceal; while the greatest confidence in the long life and good health of the present order of society in America is either openly expressed or tacitly implied by those who set themselves up as representatives of the workers — namely, the official leadership of the labor movements and the Mensheviks of all grades.

The American bourgeoisie entered the great boom of the twenties with the exuberant confidence and enthusiasm of alchemists who had finally discovered the philosopher's stone which turns everything into gold. In that golden age of American capitalism a new school of bourgeois economists came from the colleges to proclaim the glad tidings that Marx had been refuted by Henry Ford; that American business genius had discovered the secret of full employment and permanent prosperity without interfering with the private ownership of the means of production, but on the contrary, strengthening it and aiding its concentration.

They continued to beat the drums on this theme up to the year, the month and even to the day when the stupendous myth of the twenties was exploded in the stock-market crash of 1929. The very week in which the whole structure came tumbling down, the most learned articles were published in the name of the most eminent college professors explaining that this prosperity was going to go higher and would continue endlessly.

It is true that the labor leaders and the social democrats in this country and throughout the world were captivated by the myth of permanent prosperity in the twenties and were enlisted in the great parade. But they only followed; they did not lead. The capitalists were in the lead, full of confidence and optimism in those days. The capitalists and their economists were fortified in their faith by their ignorance, and that is a wonderful fortification for some kinds of faith.

They simply observed that profits rolled in and productivity increased at a rate and on a scale never known before, and that this continued year after year. Hypnotized by the marvelous empirical phenomenon, they mistook a passing phase for a permanent condition.

This misunderstanding was widely shared. The myth of the twenties penetrated deeply into all social strata in the United States and imbued even the great mass of the workers with future hopes of prosperity and security under capitalism. Those were the conditions under which the pioneer communists had to lay the foundation for a party aiming at the revolution. The confidence and illusion in the permanence of the prosperity of capitalism penetrated down into the depths of the working class itself.

The great boom of the twenties developed under the most favorable conditions. The American sector of capitalist economy was still in its healthy prime, relying on a vast internal market of its own which extended from coast to coast and from Canada to the Gulf, and on an expanding foreign trade. All other conditions were most favorable then.

But in spite of that, it is now a matter of historical record that this great boom ended with the stock-market crash of 1929. It is a matter of record that the crisis lasted, with some fluctuations, for ten years.

The salient facts and figures about the crisis of the thirties are recited in our theses. They show the depth and intensity of the crisis, its horrible effects in terms of human misery, and the irreparable blows it dealt to the American capitalist system. National income was cut in half, and with it the living standards of the workers were cut in half. Unemployment reached the figure of twenty million out of a working-class population of no more than forty million at the time.

The partial recovery, brought about in large measure by huge government expenditures, only led to a second sharp drop in 1937, a crisis within the crisis. The crisis as a whole lasted for ten solid years. And even then, a way out to the revival and increase of production and the absorption of the unemployed was found only in the war and the colossal expenditures connected with it.

And this artificially induced recovery, which greatly expanded the productive plant of the country and the numerical force of the working class, has only deepened the contradictions and has prepared all the conditions for the explosion of another crisis, far worse than the thirties and fraught with far more serious social implications.

So, in surveying the future prospects of American capitalism, we simply heed the counsel of realism by putting the question: If American capitalism was shaken to its foundations by the crisis of the thirites, at a time when the world system of capitalism—and America along with it, and America especially—was younger, richer and healthier than it is now; if this crisis lasted for ten years, and even then could not be overcome by the normal operation of economic laws; if all the basic causes and contradictions which brought about the crisis of the thirties have been carried over and lodged in the new artificial war and postwar prosperity, with new ones added and old ones multiplied many times; if all this is true—and nobody but a fool can deny it, for the facts are clearly to be seen—then what chance has the capitalist boom of the forties, that we are living under now, to have a different ending from the boom of the twenties?

Marxist realism tells us that it can be different only insofar as the crisis must go far deeper, must be far more devastating in its consequences, and must come sooner than it came in the boom of the twenties.

The specious theory expounded by the foolishly optimistic bourgeois economists in the heyday of the capitalist boom of the twenties, to the effect that Marx had been outwitted by American business genius, was refuted by the ten-year crisis of the thirties—and that crushing refutation remains in the memory of all.

How inexcusable, then, how absurd, how downright reactionary is the cultivation of this myth under the new conditions today!

In justice to the bourgeoisie and their ideologists it must be admitted that they, instructed by the experiences of the past, now take a far more sober and cautious position in their prognostications of the future. The burnt child fears the fire—that is, if he is a bourgeois economist, a businessman, and not a theoretical trifler.

The bourgeois economists and businessmen talk today far more of "boom and bust" than of boom without end. Any businessmen's economic review you may pick up at random expresses dark forebodings for the economic future. They speak quite casually—as though it is a matter of course, to be taken for granted—of an impending "shake-out" which will slow down the wheels of production and bankrupt the smaller firms which have flourished on the fringes of the boom.

At first, they referred to this process as a "shakedown," but that expressed their thoughts too truthfully. And since bourgeois economists cannot live without lying and dissimulating, they stopped talking about the "shakedown" and finally hit on the euphemistic substitute of a "shake-out."

That sounds better but it will not be one cent cheaper.

The sole chorus of optimism, where the economic prospects of American capitalism are concerned, is that raised by the American variety of Mensheviks. And that is a thin, piping chorus of trebles and tremolos, without a bass voice in it, or a baritone, or even a first-class tenor. It is a eunuch's chorus.

Our fundamental theses on the American revolution do not tie themselves to the economic prospects of the next month or the next year. They deal exclusively with the long-range inevitable outcome of the present artificial prosperity. From the point of view of our theses it makes no difference whether the deepgoing crisis begins in the early spring of 1947, as many bourgeois economists are predicting; or six months later, as many others think; or even a year or two later, as is quite possible in my opinion. Our theses do not consider immediate time schedules, but the *general perspective.* That is what we have to get in mind first.

We take the position that the crisis is *inherent* in the situation; that it may not be escaped or avoided; and that this crisis, when it strikes in full force, will be far deeper and far more devastating than was the crisis of the thirties. As a consequence it will open up the most grandiose revolutionary possibilities in the United States. That conception must be at the base of the policy and perspectives of our party from now on.

I proceed from the discussion of the objective factors in the broadest sense, as our theses do, to go over to another of the most fundamental factors making for the coming American revolution and its victory.

The American working class which confronts the next crisis will not be the disorganized and helpless mass which met the crisis of the thirties in bewilderment and fear, and even with an element of despair. Great changes have taken place in the meantime, and all these changes redound to the advantage of the revolution.

The proletariat greatly increased in numbers with the expansion of industry during the war. Millions of Negroes, of women, and of the new generation of youth have been snatched up out of their former existence and assimilated into the processes of modern industry. Thereby, they have been transformed from a multitude of dispersed individuals into a coherent body imbued with a new sense of usefulness and power.

Most remarkable of all, the most pregnant with consequences for the future, is the truly gigantic leap which the American workers made from disorganized individual helplessness to militant trade-union consciousness and organization in one brief decade. The trade-union movement in the early thirties embraced barely more than three million members. Today the figure stands at *fifteen million members of organized labor in the United States.*

One can point to this fact and say that this represents a remarkable growth. But these bare figures, eloquent as they are, do not in themselves tell the whole story, the true story. For of the three million-odd members of the trade unions in the early thirties, the great majority were composed of the thin stratum of the most skilled and privileged workers, who are the most conservative in their social thinking. The great bulk of workers in the mass-production industries—the most decisive section of the proletariat—were entirely without benefit of organization and had never even known the experience of it.

In spite of that—or more correctly, because of that—when these mass-production workers took the road of trade-union organization, with the partial revival of industry in the middle thirties, they were not impeded by the old baggage and deadening routine of the conservative craft unions. They started from scratch with the modern form of organization—the industrial union form—and with the most militant methods of mass struggle, which reached their apex in the great wave of sit-down strikes in 1937.

The benefits these mass-production workers derived from trade unionism were wrested from the employers in open struggle, and therefore were all the more firmly secured. The stability and cohesiveness of the trade-union organizations created in these struggles were put to the test in the strike wave of the past year. Here we saw a clear demonstration of the great difference in the relationship of forces between the workers and the capitalists at the end of World War II from that which prevailed at the end of World War I, a difference entirely in the favor of the workers.

After the successful termination of the First World War "to make the world safe for democracy," the ruling class of America embarked on a furious reactionary campaign to break the unions, to establish the open shop and to suppress all forms of labor radicalism. In the "Palmer Red Raids" of 1919, hundreds of political meetings were broken up and thousands of radical workers were arrested; hundreds were sent to prison; whole shiploads of foreign-born workers were deported. The newly founded Communist Party was savagely persecuted, its leaders were arrested and indicted, and the party was driven underground.

Simultaneously, the steel strike was broken, in part by ruthless violence and in part by the wholesale importation of strikebreakers; unions newly formed during the war were broken up and scattered right and left; the railway shopmen's strike was defeated in 1922. American capitalism, smashing all opposition before it, marched confidently into the strikeless, open-shop paradise of the great boom of the twenties.

The same thing was attempted, or at least contemplated, for the period immediately following World War II, but the result was a miserable fiasco. This time it was the organized workers who were victorious on every front.

The great industrial unions of the steel, auto, oil, packinghouse, electrical and maritime workers demonstrated their capacity to bring production to a complete stop until the employers came to terms. So great was the newfound solidarity and militancy of the workers that neither violence nor the importation of strikebreakers—the decisive factors in the defeat of the strikes following World War I—could even be attempted by the bosses.

Millions and tens of millions of workers in other industries, profiting by the example of the auto, steel, packinghouse, electrical and other strikes, and riding on the wave created by them, gained wage increases by "collective bargaining," while keeping their unions intact and even strengthening them.

Where did this marvelous labor movement come from? Who created it?

Here we must pay due acknowledgment to American capitalism. By the blind operation of its internal laws and method of operation, it has created the greatest power in the world—the American working class. Here is where Marx takes revenge on Henry Ford. Capitalism produces many things at a rapid rate and in great quantities. But its richest contribution to the further and higher development of human civilization is the production of its own gravedigger—the organized working class.

American capitalism, as we know, could not work the miracle of boom-without-crisis. But in the period of the twenties and thirties, working blindly and unbeknownst to itself, it wrought some other wonders which border on the miraculous.

American capitalism took millions of bare-footed country boys from the bankrupted farms of the country; put shoes on them and marched them into the regimented ranks of socially-operated modern industry; wet them in the rain of the man-killing, speed-up exploitation of the twenties; dried them in the sun of the frightful crisis of the thirties; overworked them on the assembly line, starved them on the breadline, mistreated and abused them; and finally succeeded in pounding them into a coherent body which emerged as a section of the most powerful and militant trade-union movement the world has ever known.

American capitalism took hundreds of thousands of Negroes from the South and, exploiting their ignorance, and their poverty, and their fears, and their individual helplessness, herded them into the steel mills as strikebreakers in the steel strike of 1919. And in the brief span of one generation, by its mistreatment, abuse and exploitation of these innocent and ignorant Negro strikebreakers, this same capitalism succeeded in transforming them and their sons into one of the most militant and reliable detachments of the great victorious steel strike of 1946.

This same capitalism took tens of thousands and hundreds of thousands of prejudiced hillbillies from the South, many of them members and sympathizers of the Ku Klux Klan, and, thinking to use them, with their ignorance and their prejudices, as a barrier against unionism, sucked them into the auto and rubber factories of Detroit, Akron and other industrial centers. There it sweated them, humiliated them and drove and exploited them until it finally changed them and made new men out of them. In that harsh school the imported southerners learned to exchange the insignia of the KKK for the union button of the CIO, and to turn the Klansman's fiery cross into a bonfire to warm pickets at the factory gate.

You won't find Ku Kluxers or Black Legionnaires in the auto and rubber factories today—or at any rate, not many of them. But there is a mighty sight of first-class shop stewards and picket captains who originally came down out of the hills and up from the bayous of the backward South at the summons of American capitalism.

The American working class covered the great distance from atomization, from nonexistence as an organized force, to trade-union consciousness and organization, in one gigantic leap, in one brief decade.

What grandiose perspectives this achievement opens up for the future! What are the limits to the future possibilities and powers of this remarkable class? There are no limits. All things are possible; and all things that are necessary will be achieved.

If someone had predicted in 1932, at the depths of the crisis, that in ten years' time ten million new workers who had never known unionism would organize themselves into industrial unions of the most modern type and demonstrate their ability to force the absentee owners of the steel and auto and rubber and other mass-production industries to come to terms and not even to dare to attempt to break the strikes—the skeptics would have said: "This is fantasy. This is ultraleft radicalism."

But it happened just the same.

The American workers do not always move when impatient revolutionists call them, as many of us have learned to our sorrow. But they do move when they are ready, and then they move massively.

Industrial unionism is not a new idea. It was projected long before it found its realization on a mass scale in America, and the pioneers of industrial unionism in America suffered many disappointments. In 1930, the IWW dolefully observed its twenty-fifth anniversary. At the end of a quarter of a century, the organization which had proclaimed the program of industrial unionism twenty-five years earlier was completely defeated, a hollow shell comprising far fewer members than it had started with in the bright year of promise, 1905, under a great galaxy of leaders. Industrial unionism seemed to be a defeated program in 1930. But only ten years later the majority of the most important basic industries were completely organized in industrial unions under a new name.

The workers did not move when the IWW called them in 1905. They didn't move when many of us called them later than that. But they moved when they were ready and when conditions were mature for it, and then they moved on a scale and at a speed scarcely dreamed of by the pioneers of industrial unionism.

The scale of the difference is remarkable. Bill Haywood, the great captain of the IWW—I love to mention his name—used to dream and speak in his intimate circle of the goal of a "million members" in the IWW. As a matter of fact, the organization never had more than 100,000 at any one time in all its history, and most of the time only a fraction of that number. The great strikes of the IWW which took place in its heyday, those great pioneer battles which heralded and blazed the way for the CIO—Lawrence, Akron, Paterson, McKees Rocks, the lumber strikes in the Northwest—never involved more than ten to twenty thousand workers at any one time.

But in 1946 nearly two million workers of the CIO, with only a few years of trade-union experience behind them, were on strike at one time!

These comparative figures show not growth, not simply progress, but a veritable transformation of the class. And what has been seen up to now are only the preliminary movements, the promise and the assurance of far greater movements to come. Next in order—and not far away—comes the political awakening of the American workers. That will be at the same pace and on the same scale, if not greater. The American workers will learn politics as they learned trade unionism—"from an abridged dictionary." They will take the road of independent political action with hurricane speed and power.

That will be a great day for the future of humanity, for the American workers will not stop halfway. The American workers will not stop at reformism, except perhaps to tip their hats to it. Once fairly started, they will go the whole way.

He who doubts the socialist revolution in America does not believe in the survival of human civilization, for there is no other way to save it. And there is no other power that can save it but this almighty working class of the United States.

The younger generation entering the revolutionary movement today, with the goal of socialism shining bright in their far-reaching vision, come at a good time. A lot of pioneer work has been done. Many obstacles have been cleared out of the road. Many conditions for success have matured.

The young generation coming to us today comes to a party that foresees the future and prepares for it. They come to a great party with a glorious record and a stainless banner, a party that has already been prepared for them and awaits their enlistment. They come to a strong party, firmly built on the granite rock of Marxism. This party will serve them well, and is worthy of their undivided allegiance.

This twelfth convention coincides with the eighteenth anniversary of the party. The experience and tradition of the party are the capital of the new generation. The work of many people for two decades has not been done in vain. And, besides that, the new recruits can find in a realistic examination of the objective facts many assurances that the course of development is working mightily in favor of the realization of their ideal.

Our economic analysis has shown that the present boom of American capitalism is heading directly at a rapid pace toward a crisis; and this will be a profound social crisis which can lead, in its further development, to an objectively revolutionary situation.

Our analysis of the labor movement has shown that the workers have already demonstrated the capacity to move massively and rapidly forward in the field of trade unionism; and we have every right to confidence that they will move even more massively and with even greater speed on the political field in the days to come.

The objective prerequisites for the social revolution in America will not be lacking. Capitalism itself will provide them. The manpower of the revolution will not be lacking either. The many-millioned masses of the organized workers of America will provide this manpower. It is already partly assembled and partly ready.

The rest is our part. Our part is to build up this party which believes in the unlimited power and resources of the American workers, and believes no less in its own capacity to organize and lead them to storm and victory.

4. The "Theses on the American Revolution": Letter to Farrell Dobbs

The following letter was written during the 1953 factional struggle in the SWP. It is reprinted from *Speeches to the Party* (New York: Pathfinder, 1973).

Los Angeles, October 14, 1952

Minneapolis

Dear Farrell:

I asked Vincent [Dunne] to show you the letter I wrote to him last week after your departure. Herewith is a typewritten copy for your reference. I also sent a copy to Joe [Hansen]. Please let me know the result of your discussion with Vincent on the matter and state how my summary of our discussion here stacks up with yours.

I suppose you have heard that Goldie [Geldman] finally succumbed after her six-year battle with cancer. It is good that you had a chance to see her before the end. We are having a memorial meeting here Wednesday. Rose [Karsner] and I will both speak. Did you know that she had been with us since 1930? The history of her entire conscious life is virtually a history of our movement—that part written in simple deeds by the rank and file.[98]

We are still working on the financial problem here and still recording progress. . . . We are going to keep working on all possible projects of this kind and are also working out a program of postelection activities which, among other things, ought to strengthen the local financial situation.

We are still discussing the prospects for a party discussion. It seems clear that what the party needs above everything else is a thoroughgoing discussion of the perspectives of the country, of the labor movement, and of the party. If this discussion really centers on the big questions of perspective, it cannot fail to enrich party life and create the conditions for a sound development of party activity.

I have just finished a careful rereading of the 1946 "Theses on the American Revolution" and Report—and heartily recommend this procedure both as a preparation for the discussion and for the guidance of party work in the postelection period. The Theses are a fundamental document. It is all true and needs no revision or reconsideration. What is needed is merely amplification, expansion, and concretization of the probable line of development (insofar as this is possible). I recall that, at the time, I expressed the hope that our party scholars would undertake this task after the 1946 convention. For some reason this was not done; and a mere conjunctural turn of the economic situation, effected by the artificial medicine of cold war expenditures, something like a sick heart stimulated by digitalis, was mistaken for a cure or, at least, for a long-time reversal of a chronic disease. That is not very scholarly.

The trouble is not that the Theses are wrong, but that they were put on the shelf, as if they had been merely a resolution for an occasion, and more or less forgotten. The first necessity for the party members, especially the new ones and some of the old ones, is to take the Theses down from the shelf, and dust them off, and read them. The next thing is to make all party work *and education* revolve around them. That, I think, should be one of the principal aims of the discussion in our party. In the recent period I have heard, to my astonishment, that there is a fairly widespread opinion in the party that the Theses misfired, or that they are outdated and need correction. It has been said—so I am told—that "the Theses disoriented the party," that "the political resolution of the 1948 convention corrected the errors of the Theses," etc. The prevalence of such sentiments alone underscores the vital necessity of a clarifying discussion of the perspectives of American capitalism, of the labor movement, and of the party.

I suppose there are two different reasons for the skeptical and antagonistic attitude toward the Theses. One derives from a slip of memory in identifying the Theses with the 1946 political resolution, although the report on the Theses specifically states that they "do not tie themselves to the economic prospects of the next month or the next year. . . . Our Theses do not consider immediate time schedule, but the *general perspective*." Such misunderstandings can perhaps be cleared up by a restudy of the Theses. But in order to bring this about, it is necessary to put the Theses on the table again, call attention to them, and center a discussion around them.

Another objection may derive from the opinion that U. S. capitalism is going to escape the destiny assigned to it in the Theses, or at any rate will be able to postpone it for a long, long time. Such a rejection of the Theses is serious, even fundamental, and if it is held it should be frankly stated. If it is not frankly stated, but only implied in proposals which run directly counter to the Theses, it will be our duty to explain the logic of the implications. The party members have a right to know what is really involved in the discussion. That is the only way they can learn from it.

If my impression is correct, there is a third opinion to the effect that the resolution of the Third World Congress sort of supersedes and telescopes the 1946 Theses and renders them, as an independent document, rather null and void. That's not so at all. The Theses stand by themselves; they are an essential part of any completely rounded world orientation, and are strengthened and reinforced by the world developments analyzed so well by the Third Congress resolution. I will undertake to write about this point separately.

Don't have any doubt that we agree with you about the desirability of a discussion separated from an organizational struggle. Nothing would suit our aims better. And nothing, in our opinion, would do the party more good. It hasn't worked that way up till now in New York. For the future, we'll see.

Jim

5. The Background and Purpose of the "Theses on the American Revolution": Letter to Daniel Roberts

The following letter was written during the 1953 factional struggle in the SWP. It is reprinted from *Speeches to the Party* (New York: Pathfinder, 1973).

Los Angeles, March 13, 1953

Seattle

Dear Dan:

I have delayed answering your letter of December 14 mainly because of my preoccupation with the lecture series. This is now nearly done, thank God; there's nothing left but to edit the tape of the last lecture. If I had fully realized what I was getting into when I lightheartedly agreed to undertake this series, I probably would have shied away from the project. It has been years and years since any party local got this much concentrated work out of me in such a short period of time. But I guess I got infected with the Los Angeles spirit and did more than I was able to.

I have been disturbed by one sentence in your letter where you say: "I don't fully agree with you when you say that the Third World Congress resolutions only fill out the American Theses." I have reread my letters to Vincent and Ferrell several times in an attempt to find out what gave you that impression. It does not represent my thought. All I can find is my following statement in the letter of October 14 to Farrell:

"If my impression is correct, there is a third opinion to the effect that the resolution of the Third World Congress sort of supersedes and telescopes the 1946 Theses and renders them, as an independent document, rather null and void. That's not so at all. The Theses stand by themselves; they are an essential part of any completely rounded world orientation, and are strengthened and reinforced by the world developments analyzed so well by the Third Congress Resolution. I will undertake to write about this point separately."

I think the 1946 Theses and the resolutions of the Third World Congress fit together in a completely rounded world orientation. But still they are two separate documents. The latter deal with world developments of the postwar years, which were hardly discernible in 1946, and could hardly have been written with such assurance at that time.

In 1946 the Stalinists were still deep in their postwar collaboration with the imperialists, participating in bourgeois cabinets, demanding "more production" from the workers and condemning strikes in France and Italy, and seeking a compromise with Chiang Kai-shek in China.

The immediate prospects of revolutionary developments on the world arena didn't look very bright at that time. The morale of the American movement couldn't very well be sustained under such conditions by "cheering for revolutions in other lands," as you aptly express it. These revolutions were not much in evidence in 1946. On the contrary, it appeared that the international revolutionary developments had once again been retarded and pushed back by Stalinist betrayal.

It was one of the great merits of our 1946 convention that it did not bow before the conjunctural situation and accept it as permanent. Precisely at that time, when international perspectives were none too promising, the "Theses on the American Revolution" confidently outlined the revolutionary perspectives in this country. By adopting these Theses, the American Trotskyists showed that they don't expect the workers in other countries to do all the fighting while they cheer from the sidelines.

The theory of "revolution in all other countries but our own," which is currently fashionable in a section of our party, is nothing but an expanded version of the Stalinist theory of "socialism in one country." It is a theory for analysts, observers, and commentators on other revolutions in other lands. It is a theory for a sterile propaganda circle of pretentious wiseacres, but not for a fighting party of active revolutionists. The Marxist who has no perspective of revolution in his own country is no Marxist at all.

In my New York speech on May Day, 1945, when international developments seemed most unpromising, I adumbrated the American Theses as follows: "Whatever happens abroad in the immediate future, whatever defeats and setbacks the revolutionary workers may encounter in their struggle against such tremendous difficulties, we intend to fight it out in the United States. This struggle, the issue of our whole epoch, the issue of fascism or communism, will never be settled in the world until it is settled here in America. And here it depends on the party."

For some reason this speech was not published. But I remembered it quite well and the design behind it, and found the stenogram in my files. The above quotation is from the stenogram.

This question of the perspectives of the American revolution has been at the bottom of our struggle against all other parties, tendencies, and factions ever since the foundation of our party in 1928—and even before that, in the factional struggles in the Communist Party. All the original leaders of the early Communist Party, who later split into three permanent factions within the party, *began* as American revolutionists with a perspective of revolution in this country. Otherwise, they wouldn't have been in the movement in the first place, and wouldn't have split with the reformist socialists to organize the Communist Party.

But during the long American boom of the twenties, which coincided with defeats and a recession of the postwar revolutionary wave and the restabilization of European capitalism, the Lovestone and Foster factions in the Communist Party lost faith in the revolutionary perspectives in this country, just as the Stalinist faction in the Soviet Union lost faith in the international revolution in general. It was precisely this capitulation before temporary, conjunctural phenomena that prepared both the Lovestone and Foster factions in the CP for Stalinism, with its theory of "Socialism in (only) One Country," and for their acceptance of the role of "border guards of the Soviet Union."

At the same time, it was our refusal to bow before the temporary appearance of things, our refusal to renounce the revolutionary perspective in this country, as well as internationally, that brought us to Trotsky, to the fight against Stalinism, and to the split with the Lovestone-Foster majority of the CP. Those who may superficially think that we started such an unequal and difficult struggle, and have sustained it for twenty-five years, merely for the sake of "factionalism," would do well to inquire what that fight was really about and go to the record for an answer.

The first and most important document in this record is Trotsky's "Criticism of the Draft Program of the Comintern" which was published in this country under the title "The Third International After Lenin." This document was published serially in the paper and openly proclaimed from the beginning as the programmatic basis of our fight. It shows that the real axis of the struggle, which began in the Communist Party of the Soviet Union and then became international, was precisely the question of the perspectives of the revolution on the international field, *including America.* All the other questions in dispute were wrapped up in this overall question.

The second document which I would recommend to the study of those who want to know something about the motivating origins of our party, is Trotsky's first letter to us after his arrival in Constantinople. That appears in the June 1, *1929,* issue of the paper. This quotation in particular, referring to the revolutionary perspectives in this country, should be noted:

"The work to be achieved by the American Opposition has international-historic significance, for in the last historic analysis all the problems of our planet will be decided upon American soil. There is much in favor of the idea that from the standpoint of revolutionary order, Europe and the East stand ahead of the United States. But a course of events is possible in which this order might be broken in favor of the proletariat of the United States. Moreover, even if you assume that America which now shakes the whole world will be shaken last of all, the danger remains that a revolutionary situation in the United States may catch the vanguard of the American proletariat unprepared, as was the case in Germany in 1923, in England in 1926, and in China in 1925 to 1927. We must not for a minute lose sight of the fact that the might of American capitalism rests more and more upon a foundation of world economy with its contradictions and crises, military and revolutionary. This means that a social crisis in the United States may arrive a good deal sooner than many think, and have a feverish development from the beginning. Hence the conclusion: It is necessary to prepare."

A third document which shows what Trotsky thought of the prospects of capitalism and socialism in the United States is his introduction to *The Living Thoughts of Karl Marx,* published in *1939.*

A story is going around in the party, assiduously circulated by the Cochranite leadership, that the 1946 "Theses on the American Revolution," was cooked up for the occasion to "hop up the party" with false optimism. This is the real program of the Cochranites, although they have not yet committed it to writing as far as I know. This is what the fight is really about, as I have pointed out in previous letters. Now comes the March 2 letter of Ted Grant quoting Al Adler, who gets everything straight from Cochran, as follows: "'The Theses on the American Revolution' and the 1946 convention disoriented the party."

If that is the case, the party has been "disoriented" from the very beginning. The files of my lecture notes show that on December 30, *1930,* I spoke at the public forum of the New York Local on "Revolutionary Perspectives in America" (I had given the same speech a couple of weeks earlier at the forum of the IWW). In *1933* I made a tour as far west as Kansas City and Minneapolis, speaking on two subjects: (1) "The Tragedy of the German Proletariat" and (2) "America's Road to Revolution." (Reported in the paper May 20 and June 7, 1933.) In *1935* I spoke on the same subject in Los Angeles under the general title of "America's Road to Socialism."

When I sat down to draft the 1946 "Theses on the American Revolution," I took the main outline from my notes of those previous lectures and simply brought them up to date. There was nothing new to add except some new developments and new facts. The basic line, the basic perspective, was the same line and perspective we began with twenty-five years ago.

The idea that the 1946 Theses were suddenly proposed under the influence of the strike movement of the postwar period is at best a comical misunderstanding. My motive in presenting the Theses *at that time* was directly opposite. When I first began to discuss the project with Murry Weiss and others in Los Angeles in the summer of 1946, I gave as my reason for the timing, the economic boom which was already six years old at that time, and my fears that this prolonged prosperity might get into the bones of some of our comrades; that they might take it as a permanent state of affairs and lose their revolutionary perspective. I remembered all too painfully what the long boom of the twenties had done to the pioneer cadres of American communism.

I thought it would be timely to pull the party up short with a sharp reminder of what the future really holds in this country for the labor movement and for our party. Furthermore, in my report to the convention on the Theses, I emphasized that we were saying nothing really new but were simply codifying and formalizing the basic conceptions which had animated our party since its inception in 1928 and had sustained it ever since.

This matter of pessimism about our revolutionary perspectives—that is to say, over the right of the SWP to exist and prepare for its great future—is not arising for the first time. Take my book *The Struggle for a Proletarian Party* and read my letter to Trotsky about Burnham and the pessimism of the intellectuals under date of December 16, *1937.* Take the bound volume of the twice-weekly *Socialist Appeal* for *1939* and read the four preconvention discussion articles I wrote under the dates of June 13, 16, 20, and 23, where I asserted the revolutionary perspectives in America and the right of our party to lead the revolution.

That was at a time when a section of the party was sick from the influence of another conjunctural phenomenon—the terrifying spread of fascism throughout Europe—and my articles were written to combat the pessimism it engendered. Trotsky warmly commended my articles at that time and said: "The advances of fascism are an important fact but the death agony of capitalism is a still more important fact, and that is what we have to base ourselves on."

Now the Cochranites seem to think that the documents of the Third World Congress, which analyze the new revolutionary advances in all parts of the world outside of America, have superseded our 1946 Theses and made them obsolete, even if they are willing to grant that they had any validity in the first place—which is doubtful.

Examine Bartell's unfortunate "Report" in *Internal Bulletin* No. 1 and his still more unfortunate replies to the discussion in *Bulletin* No. 2 and No. 3. Here is a man in charge of the work, and presumably of the education of the membership, of the biggest and most important local of the party, who tells the New York members that the Third World Congress has "armed us with a consistent world outlook and a clear answer to all the big questions of our time," and does not say one word about the programmatic document known as the "Theses on the American Revolution" which was supposed to inspire our work in the class struggle in this country, and which in fact has done so ever since the beginning of our movement, even before the Theses were formalized in a single document.

Is this "omission" of Bartell an accident due to a fit of absentmindedness on his part? Not at all. Bartell is one of those who think the Theses of the Third World Congress, analyzing revolutionary events and perspectives in other countries, are a *substitute* for the Theses analyzing revolutionary perspectives in the United States where we, whether we like it or not, have to do our work. Proceeding from this separation of things which ought to be united, he manages to combine in one head exuberant optimism about revolutionary perspectives in the rest of the world—which is fully justified by the present reality—with an attitude of pessimism and prostration in regard to the labor movement in this country, which has no foundation in reality.

The conclusion that a radical improvement in the revolutionary prospects in the rest of the world can coincide with worsening prospects in the United States is true only in a very narrow, restricted, and limited sense. It is true only as it affects the *immediate* activities of the revolutionary vanguard and puts extraordinary difficulties in their way; they are, in a sense, treated as hostages of the world revolution, as Stein expressed it, and made to pay for its advances. But even that is only a temporary affair, and it is disgraceful for revolutionists to let their political thinking about the great determining objective factors in the situation be affected by momentary personal difficulties.

The overall effect of the revolutionary advances in the rest of the world cannot but be a great stimulus to the mass radicalization of the American workers and therewith, in due time, an improvement in the position of the revolutionary party. In reality the events analyzed in the Third Congress documents powerfully reinforce the American Theses, and give them more actuality. The world trend toward revolution is now irreversible, and America will not escape its pull.

This is the time not to put the American Theses on the shelf but to take them down and read them, to recognize their *unity* with the documents of the Third Congress, and to make the general line as a whole, the axis of all our party work and education. My Los Angeles lectures on "America's Road to Socialism"—soon to be published in pamphlet form—have been conceived precisely in this spirit. I hope the example will be followed by others—by the whole party.

To clear the way for this, we have to settle accounts with the new revisionists who want to *substitute* the Third Congress Resolutions for the "Theses on the American Revolution" and reinstate these Theses as the programmatic guide of the party's activity.

Fraternally,
James P. Cannon

Appendix: Selections from Leon Trotsky's Writings on the American Revolution

1. From "Perspectives of American Marxism"

The following is an excerpt from a revised translation by John G. Wright of an article that first appeared in the December 31, 1932, issue of the *Militant*. It is reprinted from *Writings of Leon Trotsky: 1932* (New York: Pathfinder, 1973).

From all indications the current crisis will be a great milestone on the historical road of the United States. Smug American provincialism is in any case nearing its end. Those commonplaces which invariably nourished American political thought in all its ramifications are completely spent. All classes need a new orientation. A drastic renovation not only of the circulating but also of the fixed capital of political ideology is imminent. If the Americans have so stubbornly lagged behind in the domain of socialist theory, it does not mean that they will remain backward always. It is possible to venture without much risk a contrary prediction: the longer the Yankees are satisfied with the ideological castoff clothes of the past, the more powerful will be the sweep of revolutionary thought in America when its hour finally strikes. And it is near. The elevation of revolutionary theory to new heights can be looked for in the next few decades from two sources: from the Asian East and from America.

In the course of the last hundred-odd years the proletarian movement has displaced its national center of gravity several times. From England to France to Germany to Russia—this was the historical sequence of the residency of socialism and Marxism. The present revolutionary hegemony of Russia can least of all lay claim to durability. The fact itself of the existence of the Soviet Union, especially before the proletarian victory in one of the advanced states, has naturally an immeasurable importance for the labor movement of all countries. But the direct influence of the Moscow ruling faction upon the Communist International has already become a brake on the development of the world proletariat. The fertilizing ideological hegemony of Bolshevism has been replaced in recent years by the stifling oppression of the apparatus. It is not necessary to prove the disastrous consequences of this regime: it suffices to point to the leadership of the American Communist Party. The liberation from the unprincipled bureaucratic command has become a question of life and death for the revolution and for Marxism.

You are perfectly right in saying that the vanguard of the American proletariat must learn to base itself on the revolutionary traditions of its own country too. In a certain sense we can accept the slogan, "Americanize Marxism!" This does not mean, of course, to submit its principle and method to revision. The attempt of Max Eastman to throw overboard the materialist dialectic in the interests of the "engineering art of revolution" represents an obviously hopeless and in its possible consequences retrograde adventure. The system of Marxism has completely passed the test of history. Especially now, in the epoch of capitalist decline—the epoch of wars and revolutions, storms and shocks—the materialist dialectic fully reveals its inexorable force. To Americanize Marxism signifies to root it in American soil, to verify it against the events of American history, to elaborate by its methods the problems of American economy and politics, to assimilate the world revolutionary experience from the standpoint of the tasks of the American revolution. A giant labor! It is time to start it with shirtsleeves rolled up.

In connection with strikes in the United States — after the shattered center of the First International had been transferred there, Marx wrote to Engels on July 25, 1877: "The porridge is beginning to boil, and the transfer of the center of the International to the United States will yet be justified." Several days later Engels answered him: "Only twelve years after the abolition of chattel slavery, and the movement has already achieved such acuteness!" They, both Marx and Engels, were mistaken. But as in other cases, they were wrong as to tempo, not as to direction. The great transoceanic "porridge" is unquestionably beginning to boil, the breaking point in the development of American capitalism will unavoidably provoke a blossoming of critical and generalizing thought, and it may be that we are not very far away from the time when the theoretical center of the international revolution is transferred to New York.

Before the American Marxist open truly colossal, breathtaking perspectives!

2. Uneven and Combined Development and the Role of American Imperialism

The following is the transcript of a discussion held in Prinkipo, Turkey on March 4, 1933, between Trotsky and Arne Swabeck, a leader of the Communist League of America (CLA), on a document on U.S. imperialism prepared by the CLA. It is reprinted from *Writings of Leon Trotsky: 1932-33* (New York: Pathfinder, 1972).

Comrade Trotsky: I find this material excellent. It contains certain formulations which are not entirely clear to me or which appear to me not to be entirely exact. But they are of little consequence. In connection with the main thoughts presented I want only to touch upon the following questions:

The document is built upon the law of uneven development. This unevenness during certain periods offered advantages to the United States; but it has now commenced to become unfavorable for the U. S.

I believe it will be to our interest to define this law a little, especially because the Stalinists have treated it scandalously and still do so today. As a law it is rather vague; it is more of a historical reality. It represents the idea that not all countries simultaneously pass through the same development but that they pass through this development in different forms and tempo, etc. The law can have a thousand different interpretations.

One of the most important interpretations which leads to misunderstandings is the following: up until the imperialist epoch England had hegemony. (Stalin says that the law did not exist then and that Marx and Engels did not know it!) During this epoch the unevenness was much greater than today; we need only remember the contrast England — India of that time. The differences were then ten times as great as today. The development of India was an entirely different one from England, America, etc. But through uneven and different forms of development the capitalist world has become more uniform.

We do not need to deny the existence of the law but we must explain it. In one case I have attempted to do so by the formula of "combined development." Uneven development consists in the main in the fact that the different countries pass through different epochs. Advanced and backward countries—that is the most elementary expression of the law. Evolution, however, has also shown that the backward countries supplement their backwardness with the latest advances. From this emerges the combined development which I have proved for Russia as an example in the *History*.

In America we have another kind of combined development. We have the most advanced industrial development together with the most backward—for all classes—ideology.

The internal colonization, which is not developed in the draft material, was the basis on which the retarded consciousness of the workers existed. When we develop our theses attentively we will proceed from the law of uneven development and also arrive at the law of combined development.

It seems to me that the agrarian question does not come fully to its right in this draft, particularly in its connection with the aims and methods of American imperialism. Let us suppose that there will not be a revolution in Europe, that is, that the Social Democracy with the aid of the Stalinists so demoralizes the proletariat that fascism becomes the ruling power. It is not written anywhere that Europe must develop further forward; it can also decay. We believe that the possibilities for revolution are great. Taken abstractly, Hitler of course will not overcome the crisis. Nevertheless the decay can last for decades.

The United States displaces Europe on the world market, it becomes dominant in China and in India: as a historical perspective, as a variant, and especially as a theoretical analysis, this can be accepted just as well as other variants. China and India still offer great exploitation and expansion possibilities and represent almost half of humanity. But what will happen when capital commences its work there? These countries immediately become exporters of agricultural products. They will completely displace the American farmer. When American capital develops China and India economically, it simultaneously condemns the American farmer to death. It will produce a revolution in the agricultural world market. The cheapening of raw materials and foodstuffs will immediately increase—thanks to the great labor power within the Asiatic continent which can remain satisfied on a much lower standard of living.

England sacrificed her farmers in the interest of her capitalist development. Why should not America do the same? It *cannot* afford to do that. We have the example of Germany: agriculture is the barrier to finance capital. If the German bourgeoisie had left the doors wide open for the agricultural products of the world market, it would have very much increased the competitive ability of German industry and offered German capitalism immeasurable possibilities for profits. But the social balance in the country could not have been maintained. Hence the German capitalists need the farmers, not because of their products, but because of their rural idiocy.

That is also the case in America. When the revolution begins, American capitalism will be compelled to hang on to maintaining the farmers. But in order to broaden and deepen its development America will have to sacrifice its farmers. That is the great contradiction.

Must America pass through an epoch of social reformism? This question is touched on in the draft and answered in the sense that it cannot yet be definitely decided but that it to a large extent depends upon the Communist Party. By and large that is correct, but not sufficient. Here we come once more to the laws of uneven and combined development. In Russia the fact that the proletariat had not yet gone through the democratic school which could finally lead to the seizure of power was advanced in rebuttal to the permanent revolution and the proletarian seizure of power. But the Russian proletariat passed through the democratic period in the course of eight months; if we count from the time of the Duma, in a period of eleven to twelve years. In England it is centuries and in America also the dirty mess lasts quite long. The unevenness expresses itself also in the fact that different stages are not just jumped over but are experienced in very rapid tempo, as the democratic stage in Russia.

We can assume that when fascism in Italy expires, the first wave to follow will be a democratic one. But that condition could only last months; it will not remain for years.

Since the American proletariat as a proletariat has not made any great democratic struggles, since it has not gained or fought for social legislation, and as it remains under growing economic and political pressure, it is to be assumed that the democratic phase of the struggle will require a certain period of time. But it will not be as it was in Europe, an epoch of decades; rather, perhaps, a period only of years or, by feverish developments, of months. The question of tempo must be clarified, and we must also admit that the democratic stage is not inevitable. We cannot predict whether the new working-class stage will begin next year, within three years, five years, or perhaps not until after ten years. But we can say with certainty that the moment the American proletariat constitutes itself as an independent party, even if at first under a democratic-reformist banner, it will pass quite rapidly through this stage.

About the Communist Party: one can assert that the contradiction between the technical-economic base and the political superstructure finds its expression in the fact that we have in this country the smallest, the most foolish, and the most backward Communist Party. That is the crowning height of this contradiction. And while capitalism in America united all the advantages of world capitalism up until the very recent period, the Socialist Party has united within itself all the negative sides of reformism without having any of its advantages. (They are scoundrels without a mass base.) The American Communist Party has taken over the worst traits of Stalinism. That means that the Communist Party belongs more to the past than to the future and that the Left Opposition steps on the scene as the herald of the future. It is not precluded that the Left Opposition in America will be the first to be compelled to assume the function of the second party. We do not need to proclaim that today positively, but as a perspective we must take it into consideration.

Comrade Swabeck: The criticism will help us very much. It is not our opinion that a possibility will exist for a special development of reformism and particularly not in view of the tempo of present general developments. The perspective of European decay appears to me rather improbable, especially when we take into account that the revolution will develop in America and have its effect upon Europe simultaneously.

Comrade Otto: In Germany we have discussed this question several times in connection with the formula: advance to socialism or degenerate into barbarism. This question is still being discussed with great interest.

Comrade Trotsky: It is a question of whether we pose this perspective for centuries or for decades. If for centuries, it passes beyond historical comprehension. But if posed for decades, arguments can be found — if we assume that capitalism remains; if we further assume that fascism becomes victorious, the working class is beheaded, is demoralized, and its vanguard bleeds to death in some unsuccessful putsches; the Soviet Union falls because of economic contradictions, the crimes of the bureaucracy, and the moral effect of the victory of the German counterrevolution. We can hardly grasp what impression the breakdown of the Soviet Union would have on the proletariat. It would become frightfully demoralized. Disillusionment would possess the working class for whole generations. Anarchist putsches and terrorist acts would flare up, but the planned, organized struggles of the working class would be suppressed and disappear for decades. Large sections would famish and perish, the standard of living would be brought down to a frightfully low level. It is a decaying capitalism. We do not know how far the process can go. In this decaying capitalism there will be found forms of advancing capitalism, but reappearing in crippled fashion. The farmers become half-barbaric and masses of the unemployed are thrown on the land as agricultural laborers. However, production as a whole continues on a capitalist basis; enlarged reproduction remains, only the coefficients will not be 2, 3, or 4, but merely 1/2, 3/4, etc. In other words, negative enlarged reproduction, that is, diminished reproduction on a capitalist basis. Capitalism can return to a precapitalist basis. How long a time that would require one can, of course, not say. When Europe is thrown backward to become the continent of decay, that would naturally not mean the impossibility of socialism in America. A socialist victory in America would again have a returning effect on Europe. Combined development would, so to speak, begin a new historical chapter.

Look at Germany. In 1923 the possibility for a seizure of power existed. Since the October defeat ten years have passed by; the capitalist system experiences a terrific crisis, unemployment, agrarianization of the proletariat, pauperization of the farmers. And at the end of these ten years stands the emergence of the fascist power. This is how, so to speak, the rebound of an aborted revolutionary development appears.

Later additional remarks: The growing contradictions and difficulties of American imperialism within the world arena will not tend to weaken its power, its domination, and its economic weight as against the other rival powers. On the contrary. As in the period of growing capitalism the other nations were in a large measure dependent upon England, more so in the stage of decay will the other powers be dependent upon America.

3. From "The Political Backwardness of the American Workers"

The following is excerpted from a transcript of remarks made by Trotsky on May 15, 1938. It is reprinted from *The Transitional Program for Socialist Revolution* (New York: Pathfinder, 1974)

At present the American proletariat also enjoys some advantages because of their political backwardness. It seems a bit paradoxical but nevertheless it is absolutely correct. The European workers have had a long past of Social-Democratic and Comintern tradition and these traditions are a conservative force. Even after different party betrayals the worker remains loyal because he has a feeling of gratitude to that party which awakened him for the first time and gave him a political education. This is a handicap for a new orientation. The American workers have the advantage that in their great majority they were not politically organized, and are only beginning now to be organized into trade unions. This gives to the revolutionary party the possibility of mobilizing them under the blows of the crisis.

What will the speed be? Nobody can foresee. We can only see the direction. Nobody denies that the direction is a correct one. Then we have the question, how to present the program to the workers? It is naturally very important. We must combine politics with mass psychology and pedagogy, build the bridge to their minds. Only experience can show us how to advance in this or that part of the country. For some time we must try to concentrate the attention of the workers on one slogan: sliding scale of wages and hours.

The empiricism of the American workers has given political parties great success with one or two slogans, single tax, bimetallism, they spread like wild fire in the masses. When they see the panacea fail then they wait for a new one. Now we can present one which is honest, part of our entire program, not demagogic, but which corresponds totally to the situation. Officially we now have thirteen, maybe fourteen million of unemployed, in reality about sixteen to twenty million, and the youth are totally abandoned to misery. Mr. Roosevelt insists on public works. But we insist that this, together with mines, railroads, etc., absorb all the people. And that every person should have the possibility to live in a decent manner not lower than now, and we ask that Mr. Roosevelt with his brain trust propose such a program of public works that everyone capable of working can work at decent wages. This is possible with a sliding scale of wages and hours. Everywhere we must discuss how to present this idea, in all localities. Then we must begin a concentrated campaign of agitation so that everybody knows that this is the program of the Socialist Workers Party.

I believe that we can concentrate the attention of the workers on this point. Naturally this is only one point. In the beginning this slogan is totally adequate for the situation. But the others can be added as the development proceeds. The bureaucrats will oppose it. Then if this slogan becomes popular with the masses, fascist tendencies will develop in opposition. We will say that we need to develop defense squads. I think in the beginning this slogan (Sliding Scale of Wages and Hours) will be adopted. What is this slogan? In reality it is the system of work in socialist society. The total number of workers divided into the total number of hours. But if we present the whole socialist system it will appear to the average American as utopian, as something from Europe. We present it as a solution to this crisis which must assure their right to eat, drink, and live in decent apartments. It is the program of socialism, but in very popular and simple form.

4. From "Marxism in Our Time"

The following is an excerpt from Trotsky's introduction to the 1939 collection, *The Living Thoughts of Karl Marx*. The introduction was reprinted under the title, *Marxism in Our Time* (New York: Pathfinder, 1970).

The Inevitability of Socialist Revolution

The program of "Technocracy," which flourished in the period of the great crisis of 1929-1932, was founded on the correct premise that economy can be rationalized only through the union of technique at the height of science and government at the service of society. Such a union is possible, provided technique and government are liberated from the slavery of private ownership. That is where the great revolutionary task begins. In order to liberate technique from the cabal of private interests and place the government at the service of society, it is necessary to "expropriate the expropriators." Only a powerful class, interested in its own liberation and opposed to the monopolistic expropriators, is capable of consummating this task. Only in unison with a proletarian government can the qualified stratum of technicians build a truly scientific and a truly national, i.e., a socialist economy.

It would be best, of course, to achieve this purpose in a peaceful, gradual, democratic way. But the social order that has outlived itself never yields its place to its successor without resistance. If in its day the young forceful democracy proved incapable of forestalling the seizure of wealth and power by the plutocracy, is it possible to expect that a senile and devastated democracy will prove capable of transforming a social order based on the untrammelled rule of sixty families? Theory and history teach that a succession of social régimes presupposes the highest form of the class struggle, i.e., revolution. Even slavery could not be abolished in the United States without a civil war. "Force is the midwife of every old society pregnant with a new one." No one has yet been able to refute Marx on this basic tenet in the sociology of class society. Only a socialist revolution can clear the road to socialism.

Marxism in the United States

The North American republic has gone further than others in the sphere of technique and the organization of production. Not only Americans but all of mankind will build on that foundation. However, the various phases of the social process in one and the same nation have varying rhythms, depending on special historical conditions. While the United States enjoys tremendous superiority in technology, its economic thought is extremely backward in both the right and left wings. John L. Lewis has about the same views as Franklin D. Roosevelt. Considering the nature of his office, Lewis' social function is incomparably more conservative, not to say reactionary, than Roosevelt's. In certain American circles there is a tendency to repudiate this or that radical theory without the slightest scientific criticism, by simply dismissing it as "un-American." But where can you find the differentiating criterion of that?

Christianity was imported into the United States along with logarithms, Shakespeare's poetry, notions on the rights of man and the citizen, and certain other not unimportant products of human thought. Today Marxism stands in the same category.

Secretary of Agriculture Henry A. Wallace imputed to the author of these lines . . . "a dogmatic thinness which is bitterly un-American" and counterposed to Russian dogmatism the opportunist spirit of Jefferson, who knew how to get along with his opponents. Apparently, it has never occurred to Mr. Wallace that a policy of compromise is not a function of some immaterial national spirit, but a product of material conditions. A nation rapidly growing rich has sufficient reserves for conciliation between hostile classes and parties. When, on the other hand, social contradictions are sharpened, the ground for compromise disappears. America was free of "dogmatic thinness" only because it had a plethora of virgin areas, inexhaustible resources of natural wealth and, it would seem, limitless opportunities for enrichment. True, even under these conditions the spirit of compromise did not prevent the Civil War when the hour for it struck. Anyway, the material conditions which made up the basis of "Americanism" are today increasingly relegated to the past. Hence the profound crisis of traditional American ideology.

Empiric thinking, limited to the solution of immediate tasks from time to time, seemed adequate enough in labor as well as in bourgeois circles as long as Marx's laws of value did everybody's thinking. But today that very law is in irreconcilable contradiction with itself. Instead of urging economy forward, it undermines its foundations. Conciliatory eclectic thinking, with its philosophic apogee, pragmatism, becomes utterly inadequate, while an unfavorable or disdainful attitude toward Marxism as a "dogma"—is increasingly insubstantial, reactionary and downright funny. On the contrary, it is the traditional ideas of "Americanism" that have become lifeless, petrified "dogma," giving rise to nothing but errors and confusion. At the same time, the economic teaching of Marx has acquired peculiar viability and pointedness for the United States. Although *Capital* rests on international material, preponderantly English, in its theoretical foundation it is an analysis of pure capitalism, capitalism in general, capitalism as such. Undoubtedly, the capitalism grown on the virgin, unhistorical soil of America comes closest to that ideal type of capitalism.

Saving Mr. Wallace's presence, America developed economically not in accordance with the principles of Jefferson, but in accordance with the ideas of Marx. There is as little offense to national self-esteem in acknowledging that as in recognizing that America turns around the sun in accordance with the laws of Newton. The more Marx is ignored in the United States, the more compelling becomes his teaching now. *Capital* offers a faultless diagnosis of the malady and an irreplaceable prognosis. In that sense the teaching of Marx is far more permeated with new "Americanism" than the ideas of Hoover and Roosevelt, of Green and Lewis.

True, there is a widespread original literature in the United States devoted to the crisis of American economy. In so far as conscientious economists offer an objective picture of the destructive trends of American capitalism, their investigations, regardless of their theoretical premises, which are usually lacking anyway, look like direct illustrations of Marx's theory. The conservative tradition makes itself known, however, when these authors stubbornly restrain themselves from definitive conclusions, limiting themselves to gloomy predictions or such edifying banalities as "the country must understand," "public opinion must certainly consider," and the like. These books look like a knife without a blade or like a compass without its indicator.

The United States had Marxists in the past, it is true, but they were a strange type of Marxist, or rather, three strange types. In the first place, these were the émigrés cast out of Europe, who did what they could but could not find any response; in the second place, isolated American groups, like the De Leonists, who in the course of events, and because of their own mistakes, turned themselves into sects; in the third place, dilettantes attracted by the October Revolution and sympathetic to Marxism as an exotic teaching that had little to do with the United States. Their day is over. Now dawns the new epoch of an independent class movement of the proletariat and at the same time of—genuine Marxism. In this too, America will in a few jumps catch up with Europe and outdistance it. Progressive technique and a progressive social structure will pave their own way in the sphere of doctrine. The best theoreticians of Marxism will appear on American soil. Marx will become the mentor of the advanced American workers. To them this abridged exposition of the first volume will become only an initial step toward the complete Marx.

CAPITALIST CRISIS AND THE FIGHT FOR WORKERS POWER

Cuba and the Coming American Revolution

JACK BARNES

This is a book about the example set by the Cuban people that socialist revolution is not only necessary—it can be made. A book about the struggles of workers and other exploited producers in the imperialist heartland, and the youth attracted to them. About the class struggle in the US, where the revolutionary capacities of working people are as utterly discounted by the ruling powers as were those of the Cuban toilers. $10. Also in Spanish, French, Farsi.

Imperialism's March Toward Fascism and War

JACK BARNES

"There will be new Hitlers, new Mussolinis. That is inevitable. What is not inevitable is that they will triumph. The working-class vanguard will organize our class to fight back against the devastating toll we are made to pay for the capitalist crisis. The future of humanity will be decided in the contest between these contending class forces." In *New International* no. 10. $14. Also in Spanish, French, Farsi, Greek.

The Communist Manifesto

KARL MARX
AND FREDERICK ENGELS

Communism, say the founding leaders of the revolutionary workers movement, is not a set of ideas or preconceived "principles" but workers' line of march to power. It springs from a "movement going on under our very eyes." $5. Also in Spanish, French, Farsi, Arabic.

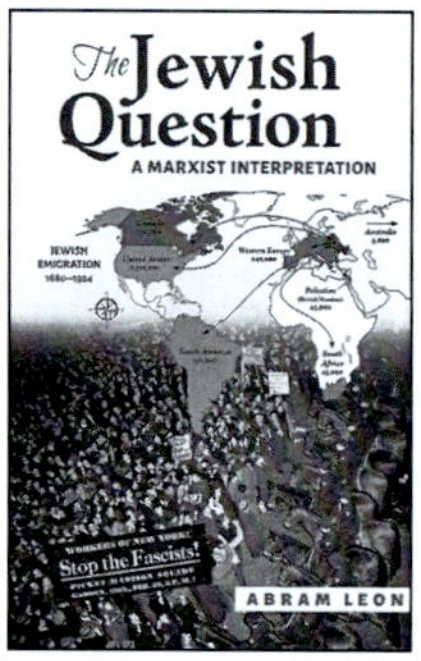

The Jewish Question

A Marxist Interpretation

ABRAM LEON

The battle against reactionary forces aiming to exterminate the Jews remains central to world politics, as shown by the genocidal October 2023 pogrom in Israel. Why is Jew-hatred still raising its ugly head? What are its class roots? Why, as Abram Leon explains, is there no solution "independent of the world proletarian revolution"? Revised translation, new introduction, 40 pages of illustrations and maps. $17. Also in Spanish, French, Greek.

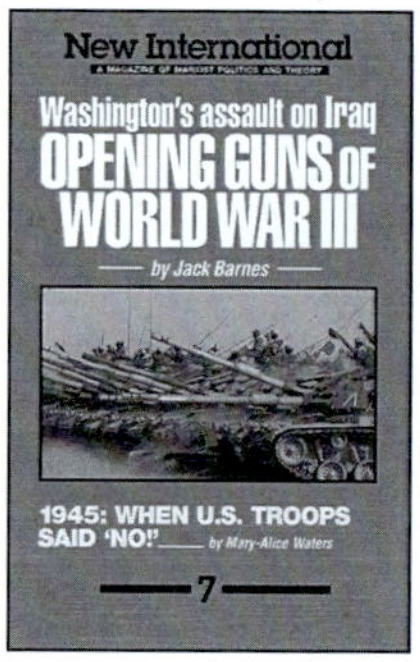

Opening Guns of World War III: Washington's Assault on Iraq

JACK BARNES

The murderous assault on Iraq in 1990–91 heralded increasingly sharp conflicts among imperialist powers, growing instability of capitalism, and more wars. Also includes:

1945: When US Troops Said 'No!' by Mary-Alice Waters
Lessons from the Iran-Iraq War by Samad Sharif

In *New International* no. 7. $14. Also in Spanish, French, Farsi.

Is Socialist Revolution in the US Possible?

A Necessary Debate Among Working People

MARY-ALICE WATERS

Fighting for a society only working people can create, it is our own capacities we will discover. And we will answer the question posed here with a resounding "Yes." Revolution is possible but not inevitable. That depends on us. $7. Also in Spanish, French, Farsi.

The Teamster Series

FARRELL DOBBS

Four books on the 1930s strikes, organizing drives, and political campaigns that transformed the Teamsters into a militant industrial union movement. Written by the organizer of these battles and leader of the Socialist Workers Party. A tool for workers seeking to use union power and advance the fight for a party of labor. $16 each, series $50. Also in Spanish. *Teamster Rebellion* is also available in French, Farsi, Greek.

Cosmetics, Fashion, and the Exploitation of Women

MARY-ALICE WATERS
JOSEPH HANSEN, EVELYN REED

"Norms of beauty and fashion are inseparable from the class struggle." That's the title of the opening chapter of this new expanded edition of a lively 1950s debate in the *Militant*, a socialist newsweekly. How cosmetics and fashion monopolies rake in profits from social insecurities of women and adolescents. Why women's integration into the workforce and unions is a major advance in the fight for emancipation. A Marxist classic on the origins of women's oppression and the working-class road forward. $15. Also in Spanish, French, Farsi, Greek.

50 Years of Covert Operations in the US

Washington's Political Police and the American Working Class

LARRY SEIGLE, FARRELL DOBBS
STEVE CLARK

How class-conscious workers have defended constitutional freedoms and fought the capitalists' drive to build the "national security" state essential to maintaining their rule. $10. Also in Spanish and Farsi.

New!

Revolution and the Road to Peace in Colombia

The Example of the Cuban Revolution

FIDEL CASTRO

"No crime can be committed in the name of revolution," Fidel Castro declares, drawing from the example set by working people of Cuba as they took state power out of the hands of its capitalist rulers. In 2008, as part of efforts to end six decades of armed conflict in Colombia, he shared the exemplary record of Cuba's revolutionary struggle with the Revolutionary Armed Forces of Colombia (FARC) and the world. $10. Also in Spanish and French.

Puerto Rico: Independence Is a Necessity

RAFAEL CANCEL MIRANDA

One of the five Puerto Rican Nationalists imprisoned by Washington for more than 25 years and released in 1979 speaks out on the brutal reality of US colonial domination, the example of Cuba's socialist revolution, and the ongoing struggle for independence. $5. Also in Spanish and Farsi.

Labor, Nature, and the Evolution of Humanity

The Long View of History

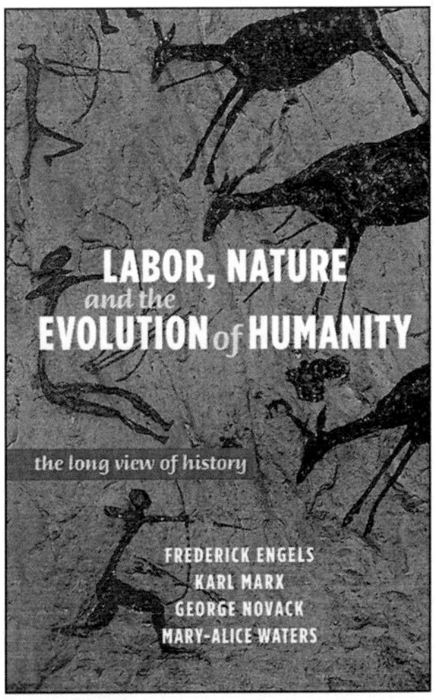

FREDERICK ENGELS
KARL MARX
GEORGE NOVACK
MARY-ALICE WATERS

Without understanding that social labor, transforming nature, has driven humanity's evolution for millions of years, working people are unable to see beyond the capitalist epoch of class exploitation that warps all human relations, ideas, and values. $12. Also in Spanish and French.

EXPAND YOUR REVOLUTIONARY LIBRARY

New!

Cuba and the Independence War in Guinea-Bissau and Cape Verde

The Fall of the Last Colonial Empire in Africa

VÍCTOR DREKE

In 1974–75 the people of two West African countries, Guinea-Bissau and Cape Verde, put an end to 500 years of Portuguese colonial exploitation. Led by a popular movement forged by Amílcar Cabral, their struggle triggered the collapse of Portugal's entire colonial empire and brought down the 40-year fascist dictatorship in Portugal itself. Víctor Dreke's firsthand account brings to life this decisive victory. $12. Also in Spanish and French.

Thomas Sankara Speaks

The Burkina Faso Revolution, 1983–87

Under Sankara's guidance, Burkina Faso's revolutionary government led peasants, workers, women, and youth to expand literacy; to sink wells, plant trees, erect housing; to combat women's oppression; to carry out land reform; to join others worldwide to free themselves from the imperialist yoke. $20. Also in French.

The Struggle Against Fascism in Germany

LEON TROTSKY

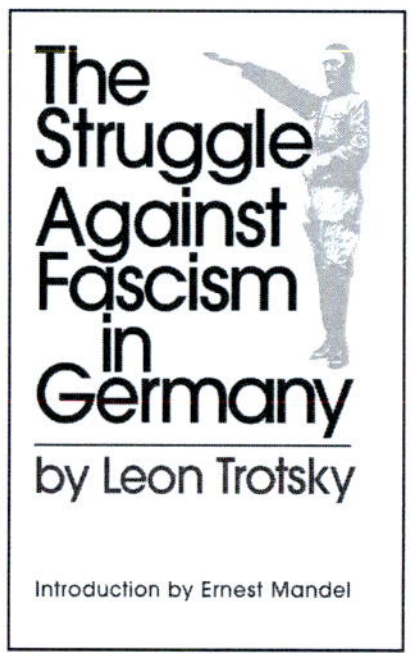

Writing in the heat of struggle against the rising Nazi movement, a central leader of the Bolshevik Revolution in Russia draws lessons from that first victorious proletarian revolution, examines the petty-bourgeois class roots of fascism, and presents a revolutionary political course to defeat it. $25

Women in Cuba: The Making of a Revolution Within the Revolution

VILMA ESPÍN, ASELA DE LOS SANTOS
YOLANDA FERRER

The integration of women in the ranks and leadership of the Cuban Revolution was intertwined with the proletarian course led by Fidel Castro from the start. This is the story of that revolution and how it transformed the women and men who made it. $17. Also in Spanish, Farsi, Greek.

America's Revolutionary Heritage

Marxist Essays

GEORGE NOVACK

A materialist explanation of the American Revolution, Civil War and Radical Reconstruction, genocide against the Indians, rise of American imperialism, first wave of the fight for women's rights, and more. $23

Imperialism, the Highest Stage of Capitalism

V.I. LENIN

"I trust that this pamphlet will help the reader to understand the fundamental economic question, that of the economic essence of imperialism," Lenin wrote in 1917. "For unless this is studied, it will be impossible to understand and appraise modern war and modern politics." $5. Also in Spanish, Farsi, Greek.

Labor's Giant Step

The First Twenty Years of the CIO: 1936–55

ART PREIS

The story of the explosive labor struggles and political battles in the 1930s that built the industrial unions. And how those unions became the vanguard of a mass social movement that began transforming US society. $27

To Speak the Truth

Why Washington's 'Cold War' Against Cuba Doesn't End

FIDEL CASTRO, CHE GUEVARA

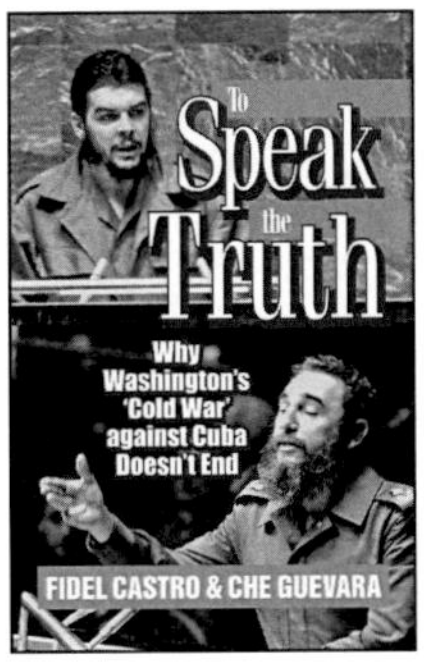

In historic speeches before the United Nations and UN bodies, Guevara and Castro address the peoples of the world, explaining why the US government so fears the example set by the socialist revolution in Cuba. $15. Also in Greek.

Fighting Racism in World War II

FROM THE PAGES OF THE *MILITANT*

An account of struggles against racist discrimination in US war industries, the armed forces, and society as a whole from 1939 to 1945, taken from the pages of the socialist newsweekly, the *Militant*. These struggles helped lay the basis for the proletarian-based civil rights movement that followed. $20

The Clintons' Anti-Working-Class Record

Why Washington Fears Working People

JACK BARNES

What working people need to know about the profit-driven course of Democrats and Republicans alike over the last three decades. And the political awakening of workers seeking to understand and resist the capitalist rulers' assaults. $10. Also in Spanish, French, Farsi, Greek.

Malcolm X Talks to Young People

"The young generation of whites, Blacks, browns, whatever else—you're living at a time of revolution," said Malcolm in 1964. "And I for one will join with anyone, I don't care what color you are, as long as you want to change this miserable condition that exists on this earth." Four talks and an interview in the last months of Malcolm's life. $12. Also in Spanish, French, Farsi, Greek.

Socialism: Utopian and Scientific

FREDERICK ENGELS

"To make men the masters of their own form of social organization—to make them free—is the mission of the modern proletariat," writes Engels. A classic guide to the operations of capitalism and struggles of the working class. $10. Also in Spanish and Farsi.

Maurice Bishop Speaks

The Grenada Revolution and Its Overthrow, 1979–83

The triumph of the 1979 revolution in the Caribbean island of Grenada under the leadership of Maurice Bishop gave hope to millions throughout the Americas. Invaluable lessons from the workers and farmers government destroyed by a Stalinist-led counterrevolution in 1983. $20

Pathfinder Press **accessible e-books** for the blind, those with low vision, or other challenges reading print books

For a list of current accessible titles, go to: pathfinderpress.com/collections/books-for-the-blind.

Visit bookshare.org for information on how to sign up.

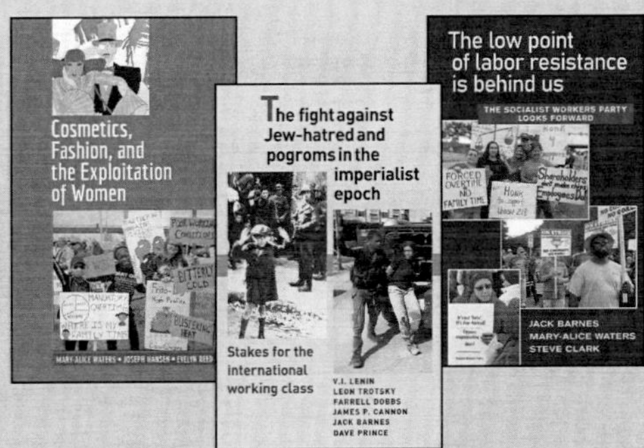

BUILDING A REVOLUTIONARY WORKERS PARTY

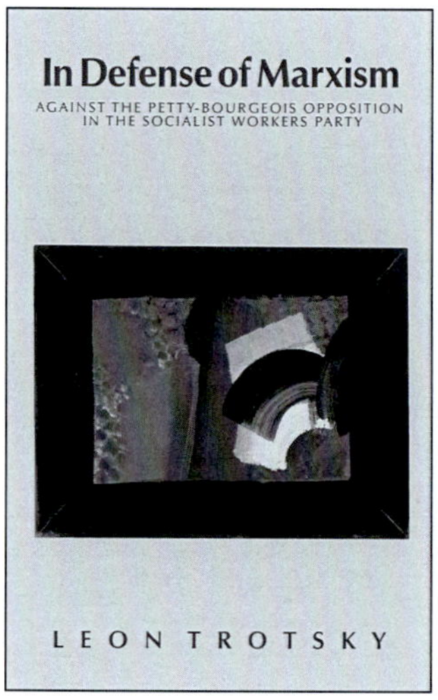

In Defense of Marxism

Against the Petty-Bourgeois Opposition in the Socialist Workers Party

LEON TROTSKY

A reply to those in the revolutionary workers movement in the late 1930s who buckled to bourgeois patriotism during Washington's buildup to enter World War II. Trotsky explains why only a party fighting to bring workers into its ranks and leadership can steer a communist course. In the process, he defends the materialist and dialectical foundations of Marxism. $17. Also in Spanish, French, Farsi.

The Struggle for a Proletarian Party

JAMES P. CANNON

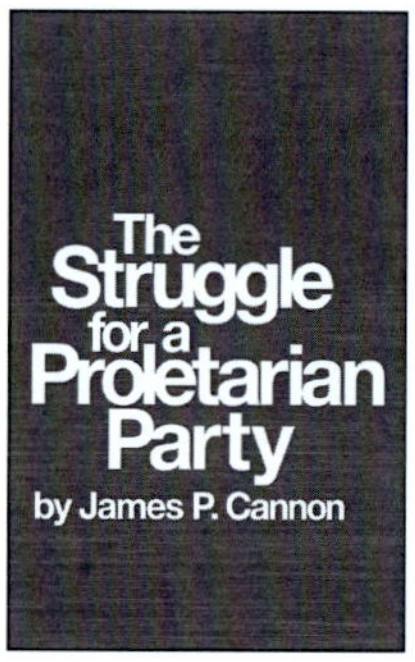

"The workers of America have power enough to topple the structure of capitalism at home and to lift the whole world with them when they rise," Cannon asserts. On the eve of World War II, a founder of the communist movement in the US and a leader of the Communist International in Lenin's time defends the program and party-building norms of Bolshevism. $20. Also in Spanish and Farsi.

Revolutionary Continuity

Marxist Leadership in the U.S.

The Early Years, 1848–1917
Birth of the Communist Movement, 1918–1922

FARRELL DOBBS

"Successive generations of proletarian revolutionists have participated in the movements of the working class and its allies. . . . Marxists today owe them not only homage for their deeds. We also have a duty to learn what they did wrong as well as right so their errors are not repeated." —*Farrell Dobbs.* Two volumes, $17 each.

The Transitional Program for Socialist Revolution

LEON TROTSKY

The Socialist Workers Party program, drafted by Bolshevik leader Trotsky in 1938, still guides communists the world over. The party "uncompromisingly gives battle to all political groupings tied to the apron strings of the bourgeoisie. Its task—the abolition of capitalism's domination. Its aim—socialism. Its method—the proletarian revolution." $17. Also in Farsi.

Socialism on Trial

Testimony at Minneapolis Sedition Trial

JAMES P. CANNON

The revolutionary program of the working class presented in federal court in 1941 on the eve of US entry into World War II. The frame-up charges of "seditious conspiracy" targeted leaders of the Socialist Workers Party. $15. Also in Spanish, French, Farsi.

Their Trotsky and Ours

JACK BARNES

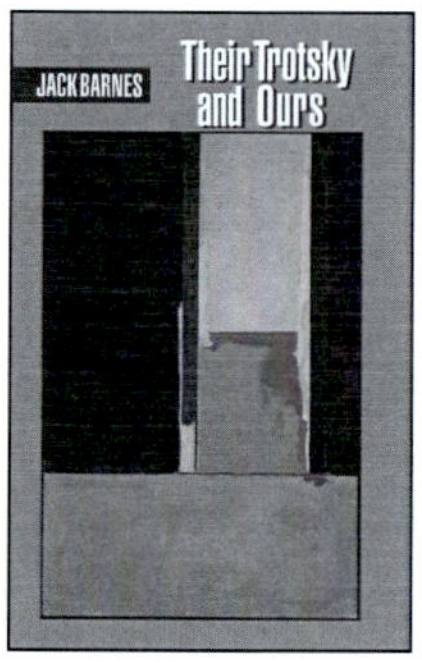

To lead the working class in a successful revolution, a mass proletarian party is needed whose cadres, well beforehand, have absorbed a world communist program, are proletarian in life and work, derive deep satisfaction from doing politics, and have forged a leadership with an acute sense of what to do next. This book is about building such a party. $12. Also in Spanish, French, Farsi.

Lenin's Final Fight

Speeches and Writings, 1922–23

V.I. LENIN

In 1922 and 1923, V.I. Lenin, central leader of the world's first socialist revolution, waged what was to be his last political battle—one that was lost after his death. At stake was whether that revolutionary government and the world communist movement it led would remain on the revolutionary proletarian course that brought workers and peasants to power in Russia in 1917. $17. Also in Spanish, Farsi, Greek.